Be The Top Gun
IN 2023!

Revenue Harvest: A Sales Leader's Almanac for Planning the Perfect Year
Nigel Green

Published by Find Evergreen Consulting, LLC, Herndon, KY, USA
Copyright © 2020, Nigel Green
All Rights Reserved.

First Edition, 2020

ISBN-13: 978-1-7343430-0-7 (paperback)
ISBN-13: 978-1-7343430-4-5 (hardback)

Printed in the United States of America

Bulk Orders
www.therevenueharvest.com

Book cover and interior design by Kailey Sullivan

REVENUE HARVEST

A sales leader's almanac for planning the perfect year

Nigel Green

Praise for Revenue Harvest

"Professional sales is about disciplined execution. Whether you're a sales leader, executive, or investor, *Revenue Harvest* will show you how to consistently hit sales targets regardless of market circumstances." — **David Brock, author of *Sales Manager Survival Guide***

"After decades of building companies, I've seen all the growth hacks and fads come and go. Nigel's no-nonsense approach to sales leadership is refreshing."
— **Michael Burcham, healthcare CEO, strategist, entrepreneur, and innovator**

"I've spent my entire career in sales and building high-performing sales teams. *Revenue Harvest* draws on farming principles that offer simple recommendations that will make you a better sales leader. This is a great read for driving sales growth with a methodology as old as time." — **Matt Tant, CEO, Relode**

"Nigel has always been a north star sales leader that I've looked to as a trusted resource through my years of executive leadership. Unlike the many sales books before it, this is truly a tactical roadmap to sales success. The sales industry needs this book!"
— **Marcus Murphy, Head of Business Development & Partnerships at DigitalMarketer**

"Nigel is a proven sales leader known for taking qualified risks that pay off. *Revenue Harvest* will inspire you to step into the moment and not let weeds grow while you prepare for the next harvest." — **Rob Waggener, healthcare executive, investor, entrepreneur, and chairman of the board of Promises Behavioral Health**

"*Revenue Harvest* is spot-on from the beginning to the end. The seven farming principles are game-changing for sales leaders." — **Jason Bristol, private equity advisor**

"*Revenue Harvest* teaches you how to build a sales team that stands the test of time. Nigel cuts through the gimmicks and quick fixes to leave you with the fundamentals needed to build a world-class sales organization. This is an irreplaceable resource."
— **Andrew Dumont, entrepreneur and investor**

"With *Revenue Harvest*, sales leaders will find a clear path to grow themselves and their businesses. Given the no-nonsense approach and clear method, sales leaders will find the support they need for consistent performance from their teams."
— **Jessica Walker, founding CEO of Care Sherpa**

Revenue Harvest: Table of Contents

Dedication

To my wife, Becky, who always encourages me to be more courageous than comfortable, thank you for always believing in and loving me.

To my parents, who modeled hard work and humility in good times and trying times, thank you for getting me this far.

To my amazing kids, Foster and Maddie Jane, who have given me a new perspective on *work*, I wrote this book for you; your future drives me.

And to all the coaches, mentors, and leaders who have helped shape my leadership and career, all that I teach and practice was taught to me by you; there's nothing original about my work.

Acknowledgements

The only credit I can take for the success I've had is that I've listened well to the following people. Thank you for your wisdom.

For providing me with opportunities and taking a chance on my ideas, thank you Bob Morales, Lee Pepper, and John Abele. You believed in me.

For supporting me when the days were long: my wife, Becky, Mom and Dad, Janie, and Carden. It takes a tribe. I'm blessed with a strong tribe.

For always telling me the truth and modeling "how things should be done," Dale Wilson, David McClellan, Marshall Millican, Roy Jordan, and Doug Hudson have always answered the phone.

Bryn Mooth made this book happen. You've been more than an editor. Your coaching and encouragement provided hope when I wanted to quit. Thank you Marylou Tyler, David Baker, and Rory Vaden for teaching me how to write a book.

To my friends who hold me accountable and make me better: thank you Andrew Dumont, Robert Crocker, Craig Young, Matt Tant, Kevin Joyce, Andrew Wilson, and Craig Whitlock.

To the professionals who have trusted me to lead them well, Amy Wilson, Jana Barbuto, Candice Campbell, Jillian Kristofferson, Tim Schurrer, Jamie Vance, and so many others, thank you. Your success makes me proud.

To my clients who share the same values, may you continue to grow and enjoy many future harvests.

And a special thanks to my friend Rory Vaden for naming the book.

Foreword

Before we get started, there are two stories I want to share: one about the beautiful state of Iowa, where I transplanted to from San Francisco in 2011 after the release of my first book, *Predictable Revenue*, and another about my colleague Mac M. These stories provide some hints about what you can expect as you comb through the pages of Nigel's book.

First, Iowa. Under the guidance of the book *Square Foot Gardening* by Mel Bartholomew, our family set out to plant our first-ever vegetable garden in Iowa. If you're not familiar with *Square Foot Gardening*, the premise is that you plant one to four seeds (depending on the plant) in a 12-inch patch of soil that is approximately six to eight inches deep. The book — part prediction, part advice, and part entertainment — carefully maps out the steps of garden preparation, planting, growing, and harvesting. The results are uncannily accurate. Predictable. Consistent.

We chose a small plot on the side of the house where weeds had taken over, carefully cleared the land, and mixed the prescribed soil recipe for our garden. As neighbors walked by, they smiled and shook their heads when asking what we were going to plant. "Corn," we said, "of course."

As the roots began to take hold, we stared out our living room window, taking pride in how marvelously our magnificent garden was taking shape. By carefully following the steps in the book, our garden thrived, and we harvested an entire summer of our favorite vegetables. The fun and practical content in *Square Foot Gardening* allowed us to strengthen our gardening muscles! The stories in the book captured the mood, spirit, habits, trends, and interesting moments we could expect during the growing and harvesting periods.

Practical advice. Fun stories. Continuous improvement over the seasons. *Square Foot Gardening* shares these attributes with *Revenue Harvest*. I know that you will multiply your results while maximizing your return on effort if you consistently apply the wisdom, tips, tricks, and actions outlined in the principles ahead.

The second story is about my colleague and friend, Mac M. A stickler for continuing education, Mac constantly includes hot seats, role playing, book reading, unique selling proposition drills, account planning, industry news, ordered sales conversation recipes, recorded meetings, and impromptu presentations in his weekly sales meetings. His team never knows when they could be called on or what they'll be asked to present, critique, defend, or implement. Which means the team is constantly prepared for any selling situation they face. Every meeting ends with one small, actionable item to put into play, test, measure, and report on the next time they met.

One notable meeting ended with a change to one of their high-performing sales conversation sequences: the ordered sales conversation strategy the team follows for scheduling, discovery, and disqualification meetings. Upon reviewing the metrics from the sequence, Mac felt Step One of the seven-step sequence (an email including an irresistible offer and educational information supporting that offer) might be better supported with a human-touch follow-up by phone. So Mac instructed half the team to continue with the current sequence (which pulled in a very respectable 25% response rate over the seven steps) and the other half to try the new eight-step sequence with a telephone follow-up call between Steps One and Two of the sequence.

This one small change resulted in a 900% (i.e. 9x!) increase in the conversion rate by following Step One of the sequence with a telephone call. When the team called prospects, they found that dozens were interested in their offer but never got around to responding, didn't understand all the ways they could achieve their desired results, or didn't know about the many opportunities and benefits that were available to them. And because the team relentlessly practiced the follow-up telephone conversation ahead of time—including exercises in conversational twists and turns, objection handling, reason-why implication dialog, and persuasive narrative—the team held these added telephone conversations with increased confidence. The team cheerfully explained to prospects why a follow-up meeting was recommended to determine fit for them and how scheduling **now** was in their best interest.

A 9x increase in conversion (what we call yield). A full five-step reduction in both time and the number of contacts needed to get to the next meaningful step (also known as cycles). All because Mac took the time to review past actions, plan a new narrative, practice with the team, and test to improve outcomes. So disarmingly obvious, yet it's amazing more sales professionals don't utilize these simple strategies.

One of my favorite things about the book you are about to enjoy is that Nigel presents a step-by-step, seasonal, continuous sales strategy that you can frequently turn to for achieving optimal outcomes in your business or professional life. Turn to any page and there are truths, affirmations, and game-changing ideas to immediately put into practice. I know you will find many of the strategies presented in this book helpful, meaningful, actionable, and incrementally profitable for you. And while I think it's important for you to chisel away at projects when implementing anything new, it is comforting to know that the book is written in a logical order (like my Iowa garden: plan, plant, grow, harvest), giving you the freedom to start anywhere in the process and spend as much time as you want absorbing and implementing.

The steps toward mastery of any subject involve giving yourself permission to educate yourself deeply and continuously. Once you dive in, it's human nature to want to become more skilled and proficient, improve your abilities, and benefit from what you've learned. Education in sales is the pathway to more business. View this book as not only the pathway to more business, but also as the pathway to a deeper connection between you and your prospects and clients, forever.

— Marylou Tyler

Preface

My wife's family has farmed a stretch of land about an hour from Nashville, Tennessee, since 1833. Over the generations the farm has changed. I can walk the land and study old equipment, retired and rusting behind a shed or grain bin. New technology makes the old equipment obsolete. Her father tells me stories of how things used to be. He's lived on and worked this land his entire life. I've always been fascinated by nature and prefer to be outside. The farm is a special place.

A couple of years ago my wife and I decided to move our family to the farm full time. After spending a decade in Nashville, it was time for a slower, simpler existence. I run my consultancy from a detached office on our land. In the morning, I walk about a hundred yards from the house to the office. It's not a bad morning commute.

I spend my days doing what I was called to do: helping executives and sales leaders build best-in-class sales teams. Running my business from an office on a farm versus an office in a city building has made the parallels of farm management and sales management undeniable. Every year, the farmer has a new number he's pursuing. It's a yield number, it's a price per unit number, it's an income number. Like the farmer, the sales leader starts her year in pursuit of revenue with a clean slate. For both, last year's harvest is done, and carries no weight in the upcoming year's performance.

Farming is hard. At times it can seem like all the odds are stacked against you. Politics, economics, weather, and other unpredictable factors stand in your way. Leading a sales team isn't easy, either. Competition, market conditions, people management, and other nuances always create adversity for the leader. Yet both the farmer and the sales leader have the same simple task: to hit a number. At the end of the harvest, if the results don't meet or exceed expectations, the reason why doesn't matter.

The world will always need farmers, and the world will always need sellers. *How* the work is done is always changing. *What* needs to be done hasn't changed at all. The principles are timeless. If you follow them, you will be successful, no matter how much the conditions change.

Introduction

SEVEN PRINCIPLES THAT YIELD A SUCCESSFUL REVENUE HARVEST

Too much rain. Not enough rain. Too cold. Too hot. The weather's never really favorable, and neither are market conditions. Despite all the uncontrollable factors, farmers persist. They don't complain. They just work. Year in and year out, they produce a harvest.

Cultivating crops isn't much different from leading a sales team.

Like the farmer, you as the sales leader face challenges largely outside your control: lack of talented staff, sales rep turnover, inadequate lead generation, not enough marketing support, competitive pressures, and insufficient product development.

In spite of these lousy conditions, you're expected to produce a harvest — increased revenue over the previous selling year.

Undeniable forces are at play both in farming and in business. Just as the seasons of nature shape a farmer's approach, the seasons of an industry or market dictate what is required of the sales leader. Experience isn't enough. Good intentions aren't enough. What worked before won't in today's conditions. The right activity at the wrong time will jeopardize the harvest. Just ask any farmer who's waited too long to get his seeds in the ground.

These *Revenue Harvest* principles are inspired by the parallels between selling and farming, two of the world's oldest professions. Managing a growing season is a study in interconnected steps and actions, all of which are dependent on the others to yield a harvest. Today's farmer has access to technology — GPS-guided tractors and sophisticated weather forecasting — that his forebears couldn't have imagined. But that million-dollar harvester sits in the barn if he planned his planting poorly or failed to tend his acreage during the growing season. He may produce a bumper crop of hay, but if he hasn't recruited enough hands to help bale it, it'll rot in the field.

Sales Is a Lot Like Farming

Like the farmer, today's sales leader has plenty of tools at her disposal: customer management software (CMS) that automate customer communication, training on closing techniques, virtual conferencing platforms that reduce travel time, and financial systems that help with budgeting and forecasting. Technology has forever changed selling.

And yet, these tools don't guarantee a successful selling year. Any number of unexpected or uncontrollable factors can undermine the sales team's ability to meet their revenue targets. Overaggressive financial goals set by out-of-touch C-suiters. The loss of a top rep or the closure of a major account. Problems with the R&D pipeline that delay a promising new product, upon which your team's targets depend. A challenging global economic climate. As the sales leader, your job is to anticipate and manage for these factors. That's leadership. And that's the part of the role you most struggle with. The unknowns. The wrenches in the gears.

If you're in a sales leadership position, you were likely elevated to the role because you excel at selling. You have the drive and grit and interpersonal skills that make you a natural salesperson. Over your career, your drive to succeed has caught the attention of the executive team. Maybe you've grudgingly adapted to the administrative tasks that *really* fall under a sales leader's job description.

And now you're charged not just with managing your own accounts, but your company's entire revenue expectation. Not just for a year. You're on the hook for generating an ever-increasing harvest year-over-year. Failure isn't an option.

Seven Principles for Sales Leaders

Most sales leaders don't have a plan (in the true sense). There aren't many playbooks on how a sales leader should approach the selling year.

Yet success at the end of the selling year depends on strategic planning **before** it begins, careful tending **during** the season, and time for rest and regeneration **after** the harvest.

We can apply seven timeless principles of farming to sales management in order to yield the revenue harvest that your team is expected to produce.

 ### Plan
The most important of the seven principles, planning requires you to imagine every worst-case scenario that may crop up during the selling season and consider how you'll deal with it. The planning phase also challenges you to interject the sales function into your company's business objectives and understand how your team's

goals support those larger objectives. Finally, the Plan principle will prompt you to rethink how you distribute sales targets to your reps — and, in fact, how you ultimately organize and manage your team.

Position

Your sales team may willingly embrace your plans for the upcoming selling year. Or they may not. Does the plan change the way they work, challenge them with stretch revenue goals, or assign them to new roles? Understand that your plan will face resistance, subtle or otherwise. The steps you take to position the plan — to gain buy-in first from key influencers and then from the full team — will make or break your revenue harvest.

Prepare

A good plan that's embraced by an unprepared sales team is a recipe for a long selling year. The Prepare principle outlines the steps you need to take to set you and your team up for success. Setting **you** up for success means surrounding yourself with the right people, properly trained, in the right positions. Your success also depends on your ability to hire quickly when a key player inevitably departs. Preparing your team means offering your reps constant opportunity for learning and skills development — not just when they first join the company, but throughout the selling year and throughout their time with you. Training builds competency, absolutely, but it should also build cohesion and culture among the group. Furthermore, it demonstrates your commitment (and the company's) to each employee and their future, making them feel appreciated and respected ... and less likely to jump ship.

Plant

The farmer who doesn't plant has nothing to harvest. And yet most sales leaders spend too much time harvesting (closing) and not enough time planting (prospecting). What's worse, some teams simply stop planting altogether; they get so caught up in managing existing customer relationships that they lose sight of business development. And that's a guaranteed path to a poor harvest, perhaps not this year, but soon.

As you consider strategies to increase your team's capacity to plant, you'll begin to see the wisdom of creating two distinct roles for your reps. The sales development rep — a role that may be new to your organization — is assigned to working the top of your sales funnel, to planting new accounts. Account reps are tasked with closing highly qualified prospects, maintaining client relationships, and seeking new business within existing accounts. You're not planting enough if your sales team is responsible for every stage of your sales process, from prospecting through relationship management.

Tend

The Tend principle may be the one that is most disruptive to your current way of doing business. It will prompt you to take actions that challenge your status quo — particularly to restructure your team to focus not on geographic territories (long the m.o. for sales teams) but on accounts. Tending well for a successful revenue harvest begins with defining the two sales rep roles as discussed in the Plant principle, and then redefining sales territories so that account managers oversee all business related to a single customer instead of subdividing that customer region-by-region. Account-based management leverages the reasons why customers buy from you (spoiler alert: their decisions aren't based on location) and deepens account relationships.

Shifting your team in this way will also alter the way you (and they) plan for the selling year and how you communicate during the tending period. In the Tend principle, you'll get the tools and concepts you need to implement an account-based management system.

Harvest

The harvest. It's the goal of all the planning and planting and tending. Sales reps and their leaders spend loads of energy on the harvest — and there are plenty of books and resources on the art of closing. Yet a strong harvest is never guaranteed.

As with farming, the harvest happens *out in the field*. It's the most intimate part of the sales process. It has to be done with care. This principle will teach you how to harvest — to close — with dignity and respect. And it will outline your very personal role in harvesting.

Restore

Farmers use techniques like rotation and cover crops to regenerate the soil after its nutrients have been depleted throughout the growing season. Worn-out soil requires ever more intervention — weed suppressant, fertilizer, water — and cultivates weaker crops. Without off-season restoration, the soil offers diminishing returns.

We both know that sales is a **consuming** profession. Client interactions sap personal energy. Travel and long hours take their toll. Pressure to exceed targets wears down even veteran reps. The sprint to the finish line of the selling year leaves the team exhausted. Yet they'll be expected to be at the top of their game when the calendar ticks over to the new season.

As a leader, your responsibility is to maintain your own level of energy and commitment, and to provide time and space for your team to restore theirs. Find the right times during your selling season to make rest and restoration a priority.

A Path to Confident Leadership and Business Results

Sales is not the profession it was ten, even five years ago. It's never been easier to identify and contact customers than it is today. Because it's so easy to find your ideal customer, investors and executives expect results — often aggressive results — instantaneously. This means that the pressure on you, the sales leader, is higher than it's ever been in your career.

But it's not just technology changing the game; the very nature of business is radically different. There's more private equity at play than ever, and the average cycle time of a private equity-backed company is three to five years. Investors seek rapid returns, which translates to escalating revenue goals. According to a 2019 Bain & Company Global Private Equity Report, higher transaction values, lack of quality assets, and increasing private equity competition are making *predictable* sales results more important than ever to a potential acquirer.

Revenue Harvest will help you manage the often-competing priorities you face as a sales leader. You'll understand how to plan for adversity, adopt new organizational strategies, time decisions and actions wisely, and give your team the resources and guidance they need … all leading to a successful harvest.

These seven principles will guide you in the coming sales year and also build your confidence as a leader. Since the beginning of time, farmers have been using these same seven principles to feed generations. Sales leaders who apply these principles will produce results, regardless of the market's conditions.

Are you ready to begin? Let's start with Principle No. 1 ***Plan***.

Principle 1

PLAN

"Give me six hours to chop down a tree, and I will spend the first four sharpening the axe."

— Abraham Lincoln

Before a single seed goes into the ground, the farmer plans for how the season will unfold, looks to weather forecasts to anticipate drought or flood, secures purchase contracts for the crop based on anticipated yield, and builds a budget that tells him how his family will come out at the end of the year.

Likewise, planning is not optional for sales leaders. It's an essential part of your job, and failing to do it can derail your career. Of the seven principles outlined in this book, the one that will have the greatest impact on your leadership is planning.

Many sales leaders don't plan at all. They want to plan, but there's never enough time. Taking the time to plan would mean less time in the field with customers and sales staff — or, more important, less personal time at night or during the weekend. Dedicating time to planning leaves you less time for your other sales leadership responsibilities.

Good sales leaders not only have a plan for the selling year, but they also dissect the annual plan into smaller quarterly and monthly segments. They also break the annual plan into team- and rep-specific plans. They have a plan for each product within the portfolio. Good leaders even plan at the account level.

Make no mistake: Planning is hard work. But when you understand its importance and learn how to do it effectively, it cannot only be the difference between hitting and missing a year's sales target, but can also elevate you above your peers. For the next few pages, we will explore aligning the sales team's efforts with the business plan, planning for the unexpected, and planning for success at the account level.

Planning Is Survival

If you haven't read Jim Collins's book *Great by Choice*, you should. In it, he explores the fascinating story of two explorers competing to be the first to set foot on the South Pole. Planning was the difference between life and death.

In October of 1911, two adventure teams made their final preparations to be the first people in modern history to reach the South Pole. For one team it would be a successful race to victory and a safe return trip home. For the other team it would be a devastating defeat, as they reached the pole only to find that their rivals had arrived 34 days earlier. This blow would be followed by a race for their lives — a race they lost in the end, as the advancing winter swallowed them alive. All five members of the second team perished, staggering from exhaustion, suffering the pain of frostbite, and freezing to death.

The explorers, Roald Amundsen of Norway and Robert Falcon Scott of Britain, were both of similar age (39 and 43) and experience. Both explorers had roughly the same distance of 1,400 miles to reach the South Pole.

In the end it was Amundsen who was victorious, beating Scott and returning his crew to safety. On December 15, 1911, Amundsen reached the South Pole. He planted his country's flag and attached a note for Scott. In the event he and his team faced an unfortunate end, he wanted to ensure credit for their feat. What he didn't know was that Scott and his team were 360 miles behind. Scott's team was exhausted and ill-prepared.

More than a month later, Scott found himself reading Amundsen's note. On the very same day, Amundsen had traveled nearly 500 miles back north, reaching his supply depot with only eight easy days to go. Scott turned around and headed north with more than 700 miles ahead of him just as the season began to turn for the worse. The weather became more severe, with increasing winds and decreasing temperatures, and supplies dwindled as the men struggled through the snow.

Amundsen and his team reached home base in good health on January 25, the precise day he'd penned in his plans. Running out of supplies, Scott stalled in mid-March, exhausted and depressed. His team was found eight months later, frozen in a snow-drifted tent, just 10 miles short of their supply depot.

Throughout the journey, Amundsen adhered to a plan of consistent progress, never going too far in good weather, careful to stay far from the red line of exhaustion that could leave his team exposed, yet pressing ahead in nasty weather to stay on pace. Amundsen throttled back his team to travel between 15-20 miles per day. When members of the team suggested they go faster, perhaps take the pole in one day, he said no. They needed to rest and sleep to replenish their energy. Amundsen planned rest. (The last principle of this book is dedicated to restoration, a principle that is often seen as a sign of weakness in the selling profession. As this story unfolds, you'll see that rest was the difference in success and failure.)

Amundsen succeeded because he planned. On one hand, Amundsen understood that he faced continuous uncertainty. He knew that he couldn't control or accurately predict his surroundings. On the other hand, he rejected the idea that forces outside his control or chance events would determine his results; he accepted full responsibility for his fate and knew a written plan would keep his team focused on the goal.

In planning his South Pole expedition, Amundsen established his base camp in a location no one else had previously considered — a bold move that put him 60 miles closer to the South Pole from the beginning. Conventional wisdom was to set base camp in McMurdo Sound; it had been used by other explorers in the past and had been proven to be a stable launch pad. Amundsen decided on the Bay of Whales. Before making this decision he reviewed notes and journals from previous expeditions dating back to 1841.

It worked.

Amundsen was right because he was the first to study the evidence and plan his route accordingly.

Scott stuck with conventional wisdom, relied on the input of his peers, and chose McMurdo Sound. He started his quest 60 miles behind Amundsen.

Neither Amundsen nor Scott knew the terrain, the altitude of the mountain passes, or what the weather would bring. At any moment, either team could get punished by gale-force winds, illness, bad weather, or an unforeseen crisis. The difference is that Amundsen knew that bad events would strike his team somewhere along the journey and he prepared for them. Scott didn't.

You are going to make mistakes in the course of a selling year. Plan for mistakes. Expect bad things to happen. Anticipate losing a key account. Know that a top rep might resign unexpectedly.

A good plan keeps you committed in the face of adversity. Commitment will produce excellence over time — excellence in the face of a bad week or month. It's not an easy thing. It takes a while to build a career. Sometimes it takes a while to get better, but it doesn't take as long as you think.

The Elements of an Effective Sales Plan

Good sales leaders plan. Despite confidence, they never feel safe or comfortable; they remain afraid, terrified even, of not hitting their number. The most successful leaders differ from their less successful peers in how they maintain hypervigilance in good times as well as bad. Even in calm, clear, positive conditions, the successful sales leader constantly considers the possibility that events could turn against her at any moment. Actually, she believes that conditions will, with 100% certainty, turn against her without warning. At some unpredictable moment, at some highly inconvenient time, things will change, and she'd better be prepared.

Let's explore the elements that contribute to effective sales planning:

- Understand business objectives
- Build a step-by-step plan
- Plan for the unexpected
- Assign the plan to accounts

Many sales leaders have a view of planning that is too narrow in scope, and that can create massive problems for the business. A good plan is comprehensive and looks at the selling year from a variety of perspectives.

Understand Business Objectives

When you approach a new selling year, it's essential that you understand the goals of the business. I doubt your CEO has told shareholders to expect the same results as last year. Even if last year was stellar, no two years are the same. When it comes to business goals, most sales leaders only think about sales targets and revenue. If you were to ask your CEO or board of directors to define business goals, you can expect a more comprehensive answer. When you think about business goals, it's important to have a perspective broader than just sales targets and revenue. Most companies have stated goals for these common metrics, among others:

- Revenue per employee
- Cost to acquire a customer
- Employee turnover
- Offering/product expansion
- Earnings before interest, taxes, depreciation, and amortization (EBITDA)
- Debt-to-income ratio

Sales leaders must align their team's selling efforts with the short- and long-term business goals of the company. If you don't adjust your sales plan to mirror the business goals, expect trying times in the future. It's not enough to build your annual plan around sales targets. Other important factors that influence the *how* of your sales plan must be included.

Early in my career, I was planning for a new selling year where the sales targets were pretty much set for me. The CEO and CFO had signed off on an aggressive revenue target. I didn't have much say-so in the revenue goals, but what I could influence was the expense budget, the resources (dollars) required to hit the sales targets. It was a time in my career where I was just beginning to build credibility with the investors and with the CEO. I only had a year (a successful one) with the company, and in order for the sales team to hit the targets, I was planning to do something the company had never undertaken. I was asking to create frontline sales managers so that not everyone would report directly to me. This request *seemed* expensive. On paper, it would add hundreds of thousands of expense dollars to the business. The CFO didn't see the benefit of the request. In a private meeting with the CEO, he eliminated it from the budget altogether. I learned of this decision during a one-on-one with the CEO. I needed to educate the CFO on why the expense was necessary. I had to go back and sit down with the CFO and explain to him that it wasn't possible for me, the leader of the team, to hit the numbers that the business needed and have all 24 people report to me. The team had grown like crazy the year before, and I just wasn't going to be able to launch into new markets, secure some of the high-level business contracts that they needed me to secure, *and* manage 24 direct reports.

A detailed budget review with finance can be a difficult process. Good sales leadership requires that you build a plan and educate the rest of the management team about what you need to be successful. Building a budget is a negotiation. You're not going to get everything you want.

While I wasn't able to get a reduced target, I was able to get additional dollars to help me hit those sales goals. Ultimately, we ended up hiring two sales managers and the business was willing to spend a little bit more money to hit that target. But it was important for me to understand how the business goal affected my team.

You need to know *how* the business plans to be successful in the selling year.

- Does the business have goals of expanding into new markets?
- Is this year's growth planned from selling a new product to the accounts we already have versus acquiring many new accounts for your existing markets?
- Maybe the business is maturing and this year's plan is focused on improving earnings over aggressive revenue goals.
- How does your sales plan support business objectives?
- You need to know what your team needs in order to achieve success as the business plan defines it.
- If the business plan shows growth from a new product, then do you need to consider building a specialty sales team for the new product, or is your existing sales team capable of

selling the new product too?

- If the company plans to enter new markets, then do you need to hire additional salespeople, or can the existing team maintain both existing accounts and the new markets?
- Will you need new resources to be successful this year? Perhaps you need to attend a conference that wasn't in last year's budget. Will you need to invest in data that wasn't required last year?

Spend time with the executive team to learn what success looks like in the upcoming year. Schedule a series of meetings with the finance and operations teams so you can *participate in* creating the annual budget. You must know the route the business will take in the next year, three years, and five years. If you don't have a copy of the strategic plan, then get one. If a formal plan doesn't exist, then challenge the executive team to create one.

When you engage with the executive team during the budget and planning season, they will see you as more than just "sales." It will build your credibility as a leader, a team player, and a strategic thinker.

Once you know *what* needs to be accomplished in the upcoming selling year, and *how* the business plans to accomplish these objectives, then you can start mapping out your annual, quarterly, and monthly sales plans.

Build a Step-by-Step Plan: The 20 Mile March

In *Great by Choice*, Collins introduces the concept of the 20 Mile March — dissecting a huge goal into incremental steps, and committing to taking those steps consistently, just as Amundsen broke his team's journey into 15-20 mile daily legs. A 20 Mile March has these requirements:

1. Clear performance markers
2. Self-imposed constraints
3. Assessment of your available resources; only keep what you need
4. Largely within **your** control to achieve
5. A time frame long enough to manage, yet short enough to have teeth
6. Imposed by yourself, upon yourself
7. Achieved with high consistency

It's important to remember that a 20 Mile March isn't just for sales targets and forecasts. You can have a creative march, a learning march, staff turnover march, or any type of march, as long as it has these characteristics.

Here's how a 20 Mile March might look for a field sales rep trying to establish a new market:

I'm committed to having 1,000 face-to-face meetings with new accounts. For the next year (50 of 52 weeks), I will conduct 20-25 face-to-face meetings with accounts that have never purchased from our company.

1. 20-25 face-to-face meetings is a clear performance standard.
2. 25 is the self-imposed constraint.
3. Since the purpose of this march is to establish a new market, the only thing the rep needs is new accounts; she won't need to meet with existing accounts to support this march.
4. Setting meetings is largely within her control.
5. A year is a time frame that is long enough to manage, yet short enough to provide a challenge.
6. She set the thresholds for this march, not her manager.
7. Assessing performance weekly will determine how consistently she is achieving the performance markers.

Take your annual sales targets (revenue and expense) and start breaking them down into smaller tranches. How granular can you get? Can you establish a quarterly target? Monthly targets?

Then assign your sales targets to each offering and different teams (even down to the rep level). Take your annual revenue (sales) goal and expense budget, break them down by month, and assign these targets to products and selling teams — this is your team's 20 Mile March for the selling year.

As you create your 20 Mile March, pay special attention to the following traps:

Account for Seasonality
Does your business have slow periods during the summer or around certain holidays? If so, then take that into consideration when setting sales targets. Don't sign off on a forecast that calls for the most sales in December if you expect (and the data shows) that the holiday season has an adverse effect on sales. Commit to lower targets. This isn't a sign of weakness; this is prudent and professional. In the Restore principle, you will learn how to use the slower periods to restore your and your team's energy, rebuild the team with training and development, and plan for the next selling year.

Be Aggressive, but Be Realistic
Don't sign off on a 40% revenue growth if you don't have the resources to achieve it. If you need additional budget dollars to hire more sales reps or upgrade systems in order to achieve a 40% growth, then fight for the resources. The planning phase is the time to ask for what you need. Don't get halfway through the year and find out that you need more capacity on the team. This will erode your credibility.

Build a Buffer
Before you communicate the plan to the team, add some margin. You want to build a buffer between what the executive team or board expects and what you expect from the sales team. This isn't

being dishonest; this is being prudent. In the next principle we will cover communicating the plan to the team, but for now focus on building a buffer into the budget. Keep the buffer at 5-10%; anything more than that isn't realistic. It's far better to miss the benchmark you've established for your team and still hit the target promised to the board. Remember that the buffer doesn't have to be equally distributed each month. As you account for seasonality, some months may require more buffer than others.

Plan for the Unexpected

Disruption is going to happen. Unforeseen circumstances will arise. How are you going to prepare and respond? If you deplete yourself and run your team to exhaustion, and adversity comes, you will be in serious danger. Don't let your team push so hard to close business at the end of a quarter that they become run down, burned out, and exhausted at the start of the next quarter. Hitting a quarter's sales target at the expense of the next quarter is dumb. Remember that virtually nothing goes according to plan; we can't possibly predict the things that will go wrong. Assume the plan will take longer and cost more than you expect.

Consistency over time is key. By sticking with your 20 Mile March in good times and bad times, you reduce the chances of getting crippled by a big, unexpected shock. Instability favors the 20 Mile Marcher. This is when they really shine.

Have you ever pushed too hard when things were going well? What happened? Did you get burned out at exactly the time when you needed discipline and focus the most? Did your eagerness ever cost you dearly?

In a setting characterized by unpredictability, with both threat and opportunity, you can't afford to leave yourself exposed to unforeseen events. Like Amundsen and his team, you too can use 20 Mile Marches as a way to exert self-control. When you're struggling to hit plan, or when you're tempted by a new opportunity, having a clear 20

Mile March focuses the mind. When you know the objective and understand its importance, you will be able to stay on track and win.

Assign the Plan to Accounts

Now that you have dissected your larger, annual sales goal into smaller incremental chunks by quarters and months, the next task is to assign the results to the team and the accounts that help you accomplish the goals. When you assign your sales target at the regional, team, rep, and account level, you will have confidence in the team's ability to deliver. If you are thinking this step is excessive, remember that it will help you as you position the plan with the team. When you can assign the sales results to the account level, it becomes more believable to the team. (If this is a new idea for you and your team, then consider jumping to the Tend principle, where you will learn the advantages of account management versus territory management.)

Account management isn't a new tactic. One of my favorite books on the subject, *New Successful Large Account Management* by Robert Miller and Stephen Heiman, was written in 1991. Sales teams that implement account management have deeper relationships with their customers (in fact, many customers will view your business as an extension of theirs), have a better understanding of where the business is being generated, and more consistently deliver at or above forecast.

In its simplest form, the sales territory is *an area of responsibility for an individual or team of salespeople by which sales are expected.* Not Los Angeles. Not mid-market. Not the Midwest. So why do we build sales plans based on geography? Is that the best way to realize and measure opportunities for the business? The geographical territory model is no longer the optimal structure for planning sales results. More importantly, it doesn't create value for customers. Many companies have moved away from a geographical territory model because it no longer places the sales team in a position to win the most market share. It confuses the team and it confuses the customers. Eliminate the imaginary geographical boundaries and assign the sales results from your plan to accounts. Once you shift away from a geographical territory model to an account management model, your team's performance will improve.

Account Management vs. Territory Management

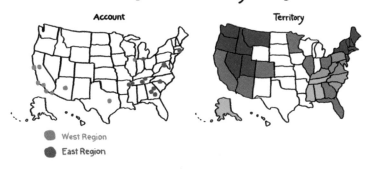

Account management = reps are assigned to a group of companies, regardless of location
Territory management = reps are assigned to a geographical region

If your company still utilizes a territory model, then let this be the year you break away and start to see powerful sales growth. The territory model limits a leader's ability to develop new business, which diminishes scale and traction at the rep level. Territory management is also one of the most common barriers to your ability to deliver the results expected in the plan, because some reps (and teams) end up with too few opportunities, some reps (and teams) have too much opportunity to manage. The leader thinks the rep (territory) is performing well (or poorly) without any insight into how much business is being lost, overlooked, or undercapitalized.

- Territory management is often a sign of lazy or poorly thought-out management control.
- It skews a manager's ability to measure a salesperson's *true* abilities.
- Customers outside the defined territory are missed or don't get developed, and the business suffers as a result.

Look at last year's results by account:

- Can you expect last year's top accounts to buy even more this year?
- Which accounts' sales volumes were surprising (higher or lower than expected)? How does that affect your plans?
- How many more new accounts do you need to hit the growth goals?
- If you have a new product to sell, how many existing accounts can you expect to buy the new product? Or do you need a new type of account to buy the new product?

We will do a deeper dive on account management in the Tend principle. For now, it's important to take your sales results and assign them to your accounts. By month, by quarter, and by year, assign believable sales quotas to the accounts that you can rely on to hit your targets.

A poor sales team structure makes good performance impossible, no matter how good the sales leader or sales plan may be.

Would You March?

In the next principle, we will discuss positioning the plan. Positioning is about: 1) creating buy-in on the plan and 2) moving resources (including people) into the best position for success in the selling year.

- Before we talk about how you'll position your plan to the team, make sure that the executive team has approved it. Equally important, ask yourself: *Is this plan believable?*

- Look at it from every possible angle. If you were a sales rep, would you be excited or scared? How will your sales managers react when they see the plan for the first time? Try to anticipate what each role's perspective will be on the plan. Here are some questions to consider:

- Is the monthly distribution of results attainable? Are you being too aggressive in early months when you have too many new sales reps who aren't yet well-established in the business?

- Conversely, are you exposing the team to really aggressive goals late in the year, that could be more attainable by shifting some results to earlier in the year?

- How does your cost per sale trend over the year? Does it get better or worse? How does this metric compare to last year's? How does the trend align with the company's financial goals?

- How does revenue per employee trend over the selling year? How does it compare to last year?

- What key business goals will be accomplished as a result of successfully executing this plan? Will any business goals be adversely affected or overlooked?

Now let's *position* the team to march.

Principle 2

POSITION

"Individual commitment to a group effort — that is what makes a team work, a company work, a society work, a civilization work."

— Vince Lombardi

Farmers understand what grows well in their soil and climate: tomatoes don't grow in Alaska; wine grapes grown in Bordeaux taste different from those grown in the Napa Valley. Planning for a growing season without positioning the crops in the proper conditions is an exercise in futility.

The process of presenting the upcoming year's sales plan is *positioning*. Positioning your sales team is about creating the right conditions to cultivate success and getting everyone moving in the right direction so that your efforts yield a strong harvest.

Not only does positioning set the course for the upcoming year, but it also is a way to re-center the team on company mission and values. It's not enough to have a good sales plan that has realistic growth expectations. A good sales plan poorly positioned will result in a bad year. Yet sales leaders are quick to dismiss the importance of positioning, simply telling their reps what their targets are without building buy-in. This practice doesn't work well. It's the sign of management, not leadership. Positioning is the first step of execution.

How Positioning Can Catalyze Growth

In 2012, I took a position as the head of sales for Foundations Recovery Network, a mental health and substance use disorder treatment provider. I joined the team late in the year, and the 2013 sales targets had already been set. Honestly, since I was so new to the organization and had no industry experience, I had no way of knowing if the targets were realistic or not. I trusted the leadership team that set them and I trusted my ability to lead ... well, **sometimes** I trusted myself.

What I did know was that the team I was tasked to lead hadn't hit a sales target in a long time, and they weren't sure about me and my leadership capability.

I was smart enough to know that if I took the 2013 sales plan and started assigning targets to the team members, I would face a mutiny. Since they hadn't historically hit their targets, how could they possibly believe the larger 2013 targets were achievable?

So I brought the team together in November for a meeting. For two days, I positioned the 2013 sales targets in a way that would create buy-in and excitement about the future. I was nervous because the team didn't know me well and I didn't know them well. Time wasn't my friend, and there was no way to ease up on the targets.

We spent the first half of day one talking about the mission of the company. They heard firsthand from our CEO about why this mission was important to him. Some of the salespeople shared their own personal stories of overcoming addiction and mental health issues. We brought in a couple of our accounts to share how working with Foundations made their business better. They told us how we were different from the competition. Finally, we heard a few testimonials from past patients who were recovering and living life well.

By lunchtime it was clear that Foundations didn't just exist to be an addiction treatment provider, but rather it is the leader in evidence-based treatment for patients struggling with co-occurring mental health and substance use disorders. A strong, bold mission.

Excitement was building. Everyone knew they were in the right room, working for the right company, pursuing a noble mission. At this point, we hadn't even mentioned sales targets.

After lunch, we started a conversation about the future. About a compelling vision for what the world could look like if we accomplished our goals.

- How would the world be a better place if we treated more patients?
- What does success look like for our customers, the healthcare professionals who refer their patients to us?
- What's the benefit to the company if we succeed? To the team?
- How would each team member's life be better as a result?

Each person on the team had something to share. Without exception, everyone had a personal goal that would be met if the company was successful.

Everyone believed the future would be better than today. Everyone knew we had work to do, and yet everyone bought in.

We used elements of everyone's ideas for a preferred future to develop a vision statement: *Further, Faster.*

Those two words represented everything for the team, the customers, the patients, and our company.

Further

We knew that in order to realize our vision of the future and mission of the company, we needed to further penetrate the market. We needed to go deeper with our existing accounts, exploring how we could help them succeed in their businesses.

We needed more accounts too. We knew we would need to expand our presence into new markets and new call points. We had to be willing to go the extra mile to be successful: one more meeting a day, one more new account a week. To push further than we were comfortable.

Faster

We knew we had to work fast. When the service you provide is a matter of life or death for the patients, there's no time to waste. At that time, more than 20 million Americans were suffering, in silence, from an addiction — and we had to reach them. In order to move fast, we needed a sense of urgency that didn't currently exist. The team challenged one another to pick up the pace.

So there we were at the end of the first day. Further, Faster. Everyone was ready to march.

That's when I told the team that it was a dream and not a vision until it was measurable. They understood. The team was now in the right position to see the plan.

We spent all of the second day working on the plan. I showed the team the targets for 2013. The targets were big, especially at the end of the year. The targets in the plan made the vision measurable. It gave us clarity on how well we were doing at moving the business from here to there.

I walked them through all the elements of the plan:

– How it supported our mission
– How it aligned with our newly stated vision
– How we were going to reorganize in order to succeed
– What each of them stood to gain as a result

They marched. We hit our targets in 2013. Adversity came as we expected. Some people left. New teammates joined us on the mission. It was a hard year, everyone agreed. Most of the team stayed with the company for many years. We went on to triple the size of the business in three years, never missing an annual sales target along the way.

Without exception, we finished every year planning and positioning for the next selling year. Mission. Vision. Plan.

Brace for Resistance

At this point you've built the sales plan with the management team. You've worked hard to create a stepwise sales plan that:

1) Is strenuous but realistic
2) Accounts for seasonality
3) Anticipates adversity
4) Supports the goals of the business

But you haven't yet presented it to the sales team. You probably have mixed feelings about presenting the plan, because you remember what it felt like as a rep to receive the upcoming year's sales plan. You know that not everyone is going to have the same excitement or acceptance about what the plan represents. Let's face it: The upcoming year will provide some reps with more opportunity than others. The plan will require everyone to do something differently. You can do a quick mental run-through of the team and identify how each person might react. You also know that in order for the plan to be successful, the team will need to deliver on each month's targets. Will they be excited about the new plan, or will they resist or fear it?

Any new sales plan represents change. Each team member will respond to the new plan differently. Some will see how the changes can be good for them personally; others will feel uneasy about them. Because they are human, they will initially focus on how the changes will affect them. Don't expect your team to see the bigger picture: how the plan helps the company accomplish its mission and how it will provide an opportunity for career advancement for each member of the sales team.

How you position the sales plan is more important than the elements of the plan.

As you approach your selling year, make sure everyone and everything is in the right position so that you can capitalize on every opportunity. You will likely need to put people in different roles. Promotions. Terminations. Lateral moves to new products or new markets. You've already made these changes in the plan, and now it's time to communicate the changes to the team. But you can't just schedule a conference call and jump right into the numbers.

Most sales leaders rush to share the plan with the team as soon as it's been approved by leadership. Often, that's because they didn't allow adequate time to complete the plan before the new selling year began, so every day the leader delays presenting the plan, the team falls farther behind goal. Rushing to publish an overdue sales plan will make positioning even harder. You will create more anxiety than you alleviate.

The Plan's Success = The Team's Success

The first objective of positioning is showing the team where you're taking them — and what's in it for them personally. The sales plan is the team's turn-by-turn navigation, not just for the selling year but also for each of their careers. Remember that the younger generations have different motivations than the older generations. Know what motivates your team. The most important element of positioning is creating buy-in to the plan at all levels of the sales organization. Buy-in is created by attaching the results of the plan to the goals of the individuals on the team.

Even though you ultimately want buy-in to the plan, you can't start by presenting the numbers.

- If the team doesn't understand why the plan exists, then they won't budge.
- If the team doesn't think the plan is achievable, then they won't push themselves to work hard.
- If the team doesn't see how the plan benefits them, then they won't march.
- If all the hard work required in the upcoming year doesn't support a noble mission bigger than the individuals, then the plan will fail.

Often, sales leaders present the upcoming year's sales targets without doing the important work of positioning. A simple positioning formula is the best way to get the team to not only accept the sales plan, but also to own it as if they created it themselves. Good positioning is formulaic, step by step.

Positioning: A Fail-Proof Formula

The fail-proof formula for positioning your sales team for success is:

Mission, then Vision, then Plan

Don't begin with the sales targets.

Positioning is like laying steppingstones across a rushing river that stands between here (now) and there (a preferred future).

The team may see the other side of the river and agree that the other side of the river is better, but without the stones (the plan) there's no way to reach the destination.

Let's further explore the elements of the formula: mission, vision, plan.

– **Mission** is the company's nonnegotiable imperative. It's where we are now (this side of the river). It's why the company exists. It's the founder's story. It's about the problem you solve for your accounts. It's the company's sales pitch. Mission is bigger than any one-, three-, or five-year strategic plan. Why are we here? What problems do we solve for our customers?

– **Vision** is where the mission takes you (the other side of the river). It's what the world looks like after you've solved a problem using your company's offering. Vision is always measurable. Vision is also about how the sales team communicates the mission to the market. A powerful vision can be reduced to a few words or a sentence to characterize how the sales team accomplishes the mission.

– **Plan** is the stepwise sequence of results that leads to success in the selling year. It's the sales plan for the year broken down into your 20 Mile March.

Your job as the leader is to get the team to succeed in supporting the company's mission and vision. The sales plan, properly positioned, represents the stones used to reach the other side. The emphasis needs to be on the other side, not the stones. The plan is just a tool to accomplish the vision (reach the other side). Present the monthly targets as merely stones that lead to the other side of the river. Without demonstrating the importance of mission and vision before the business goals, you've just got a pile of stones — and that doesn't make much sense to the team.

Step 1: Identify the Mission

The business has had success; that's evident by your account base and the fact that you have a sales team. But your CEO and board of directors still think there's more to accomplish. That's why the sales plan shows growth.

In order to be successful in the upcoming selling year, your sales plan is going to ask the team to do something differently. To produce results that maybe haven't been seen before. Some reps are going to have targets bigger than they could ever imagine. You're going to ask your team to change the way they approach your market and change the way they serve this organization. In other words, you're going to ask them to change what they do and how they do it, every day. Here are some typical changes your plan may include:

- Higher sales targets
- New, unproven offerings with aggressive goals
- Restructuring of teams and roles
- Changes to the team's makeup: people we care about leave; new, unknown members will or have already joined the team

The resistance you will face is not to the plan *but to having to act differently*. Change can create chaos. It's uncomfortable. Your team will resist change because it requires them to do something differently. Resistance isn't to an idea; it's to doing things differently. This is why you must lead your positioning with the mission. A mission gives meaning to pain and sacrifice.

Building a business is hard work and requires a certain moxie to overcome challenges and adversities. Pain, sacrifice, challenges, and adversity aren't attractive characteristics of a business opportunity — *unless you know and are passionate about the mission of the company*. Mission is bigger than the individual. Mission creates community by bringing together a collective of people committed to solving the same problem.

Most sales professionals spend their career selling or seeking to sell a noble offering — an offering, and a company, that elevates the significance of the work and their individual contribution to solving a problem. The nobility of the company's mission makes the pain and sacrifice worth it. Enduring the struggles with a team that's committed to the same cause is more powerful than any motivation a sales leader can create. A clear mission is a sales leader's tool to move a team forward in the face of adversity.

Answer the following questions as you define this side of the river:

- How clearly can you and your team articulate the mission of your company?
- How many teammates work here primarily because of the mission versus they love the compensation plan?

- Can you reference real-life examples of your company's mission delivering success to your accounts?
- What are you ultimately here to do?
- Knowing the answers to these questions is an essential responsibility of leadership.

To properly position and lead your sales team, you and the team have to fall in love with the mission and the vision. Too many leaders and teams fall in love with plan. When the plan changes — and it will — they are exposed. Tactics like using your current compensation plan as a tool to woo talent is leading with the plan, and when the compensation plan needs to change to support the business, where does that leave the sales rep that came aboard only because of the lucrative compensation plan? You'll lose the team. Keeping the team focused on the mission and vision, and only mildly infatuated with the plan, allows for easy pivoting when the plan needs to change.

Step 2: Create a Compelling Vision of the Future

"Vision is the most potent offensive weapon in a leader's arsenal. Vision is a picture of the future that creates passion in people." — Bill Hybels

Vision moves people. It gets them out of bed in the morning. A compelling vision makes the mission a nonnegotiable. If we don't succeed, then people will suffer. Vision characterizes the upside of all the pain required to accomplish the mission. Vision is the future state where the mission has been accomplished and the injustice has been resolved.

- What is your company's and customer's preferred future?
- What does the world look like when you accomplish the mission?

Vision has to be measured or it's just a dream. My friend Ryan Deiss and his company DigitalMarketer have a vision to double the revenue for 10,000 companies over the next five years.

That's a measurable vision. If you were to ask him, he'd be able to show you an annual sales plan that shows stepwise performance expectations to support that vision. But he cares more about the vision than the plan.

Use the vision as a branding tool. At Foundations Recovery Network, we took our vision statement — Further, Faster — and put it in our email signatures. We had shirts and bags and other materials made. We even named our sales meetings "Further, Faster Summits."

This kept the vision front and center. "Further, Faster" became a self-governing tool. If a rep wasn't pulling his weight, he could expect a teammate to challenge him to go further, faster.

Step 3: Use the Plan to Make the Vision Measurable

Mission drives the vision, which drives the plan. You don't change the mission; you alter how you reach it. The sales plan is full of small changes to the team's structure, but the mission and vision remain the same. Ultimately, change has to take place at the plan level if you are to be successful in the selling year. You can expect the most resistance to the plan. People are more open to change when they see it in the broader context of the organization, the mission and vision.

Framing the Plan

How will you frame the upcoming year in relation to last year's results? Are you leading in an upturn, status quo, or downturn? Each situation requires a different approach:

Downturn
In a downturn we have to declare an emergency, create a plan, and implement it fast. Seasoned leaders have to come up with a signal for a code red. Everyone has to pull together fast if the business is burning.

Does a downturn mean you are a terrible leader? If you lead long enough, you will experience all three realities. Internal and external circumstances will lead you to the results. When you see a downturn, create a code red.

Status Quo
What about a sleepy team? Then you have to spark a fire. Status quo is not acceptable. Status quo is dangerous. Growth is required; healthy beings, including companies, always grow. A sleepy sales team is a precursor to sure demise. Start a raging fire. Take a risk with younger leaders, let them play more.

Upturn
What about when you are setting records? Are you creating career advancement for your team? Is the sales team enjoying and celebrating success, or do they see you as a ruthless taskmaster? Are you resting on your laurels? Remember: Nothing fails like success.

Your whole team knows what reality you are in, so you have to speak with honesty and candor. They are all waiting on you to wake up and realize the situation, and then lead them out of it.

What is your current reality? Down? Up? Status Quo?

- Where is the business in its life cycle? A startup building on momentum or an established company preserving market share?
- What role will the sales team play in the upcoming year?
- Do they understand the importance of their individual contribution to the larger mission?

Leverage Influence to Achieve Impact: The Sales Council

"Leaders have followers. Managers have employees and quotas. Managers sell stuff. Leaders create opportunities and make new realities possible."
— *Seth Godin*

Influencers are people who have the ability to affect the decisions of others. Your team includes a select few influencers. Think about it for a minute: Who are the people on your team that have a way of affecting how the rest of the team thinks and acts? Selecting *influencers* from each level of the sales organization is a great way to position the sales plan for success. Use these influencers — leaders in their own roles — as supporters to get buy-in from the entire team.

A council is a *group of people who come together to consult, deliberate, and make decisions.* A Sales Council can help you not only position your annual plan with the team, but also to advise you on ongoing decisions. The strongest leaders don't go it alone; they make informed decisions based on the input of experts. Individuals who have influence and credibility among the team can help grease the wheels for change and can motivate others throughout the year.

When you gather this group, do it in a formal, transparent manner. Choose people you can rely on. Give it a name, a structure, a regular meeting schedule, and an agenda.

Who Is On It

Often, leaders go to the wrong sources when they seek counsel. They get caught up in bureaucracy and hierarchy. They ask the people they *think* they should ask. A Sales Council gathers all the right people at your decision-making table. Who can help you make better, smarter decisions, regardless of their title and tenure? These are the people you want on your council.

That means looking not just at your top lieutenants, but at others across your team and the corporate organization. Frontline sales reps, customer support reps, and other personnel that don't report directly to you. Up-and-comers who would benefit from exposure to higher-level conversations and whose energy you can leverage. Veterans who've built solid relationships with customers, and new reps who've shown potential. People who can play against your own weaknesses and biases.

Andy Stanley, author of *Next Generation Leader*, once said, "Time in an organization dilutes your awareness of the way things really are." So the longer you've been in this role, the longer you've been with the company, the less likely you are to see things for what they really are.

You might feel like this is going to ruffle some feathers. It will. People will wonder why you've chosen certain colleagues over them. Let the team know you've selected the council for a reason, that it's not necessarily forever, but it's designed to help you make the best decisions for the team.

Let the Council See the Plan First

The first item on the agenda for the Sales Council is reviewing the upcoming year's sales plan. A key role for this group is to champion new ideas, rally the team's support, and create change. That's why it's essential to gather people across hierarchical levels and job functions.

Your counselors can tap their relationships with others to help pull everyone along, even in challenging times. They can identify potential roadblocks and objections and help you build a plan for overcoming them. They also represent the breadth of the team's perspective on many issues that affect the business, across areas you may not be deeply familiar with. How will a sales push on a new product affect customer service? Production? Does the company have the capacity to fulfill orders your team's out there selling?

Walk them through the annual plan and all of its elements:

- Sales targets (by month, by product line, by rep, by team)
- Monthly expense targets
- Newly available resources
- Product launches
- Hiring needs or shifting roles

Get honest feedback on whether or not the plan will fly. Listen to the council. Ask more questions than you think you should. Gather as much feedback as possible. Take good notes of what you hear. Once everyone on the council supports the plan, then it's time to communicate it to the rest of the team — along with any aggressive goals or reshuffling of roles. Rely on this group of influencers to explain the *whys*: why the changes are happening, why they matter, why decisions were made.

Ongoing Guidance
While the Sales Council will help you gain buy-in for the plan, it's also an effective ongoing resource for your own decision-making. Meet with them monthly, with a set agenda that includes all of the factors that are affecting your business, from finance, legal, product, succession planning, sales. When you're faced with a significant or difficult decision, this group of advisors can help you overcome your own biases, hone in on the truth, and consider a diverse range of opinions. Council members will represent their departments and their roles within the sales function, so that when you're considering tough decisions, you understand how they'll affect the broader organization.

Sales Plan Kickoff

The best way to position a sales plan is to have a kickoff meeting, either before the selling year starts or at the very beginning of the selling year. (Of course, you'll need to budget appropriately for this meeting; if the size or location of your team makes an in-person meeting unrealistic, then schedule a virtual one.) Sales kickoffs are a significant investment for the business and especially for you, the sales leader. They require extensive planning to be successful.

A good sales kickoff meeting serves as a segue from the principles of Positioning to Preparing. The first half of the meeting is positioning to secure buy-in on the plan, and the second half of the meeting is training that prepares them to succeed in the upcoming year. But it's more than just a segue from Positioning to Planning. In fact, great kickoff meetings cover all seven of this book's principles.

Rightsizing the Kickoff Meeting

The scale and scope of your sales kickoff meeting must match with the size and stage of your company. If you're a 10 person sales team where everyone lives within driving distance, then a sales kickoff could be a day at a lake house having food and drinks while discussing the year's upcoming plan. If you're an international company with sales reps from across the globe, then maybe you can use the meeting as an international vacation where you visit a different country each year. Companies of this size can overtake an entire hotel for a week.

It's up to you to know what scale your company can accommodate. Regardless of what you decide, there are some nonnegotiables for every kickoff meeting:

1. Don't do it in the office (you can visit the office if there are people who need to see it).
2. Make sure the executive team plays a role in the content and attends the event.
3. You need a budget. It is not cheap; there is opportunity cost involved as well, as every day spent in a meeting room is a day lost in the field with customers.
4. It has to be fun. Do something that will create memories. Take the team to a sports event. Do a team-building exercise. Raft a river. Go on a hike. Get creative and do something memorable.

Thinking Through Meeting Details

Your sales kickoff is a mix of keynote speeches, breakout sessions, and workshops all designed to position the sales plan and prepare the team to march. You need to make sure you've incorporated content that not only presents and positions the sales plan, but also covers all the principles in this book. Each agenda item needs to support a principle.

Planning — Reveal the year's sales plan with stepwise benchmarks.

Positioning — Recap and clarify the company's mission and vision. This can be covered by you or another executive who is admired and respected by the team.

Preparing — Provide relevant training on product, market, craft, etc. Leverage subject matter experts to train on the topics your team needs most. If they don't exist within the organization, bring in outside resources (consultants and trainers).

Planting — Launch strategic initiatives and joint ventures. Sometimes it makes sense to have representatives from strategic accounts or partner companies join the meeting for a particular agenda topic.

Tending — Present concepts and training on how to manage the business. This is an opportunity to let your sales managers or top performing reps teach business management concepts to the team.

Harvesting — Provide targets, quotas, closing expectations, and objectives. Reserve time for some sales reps (all reps for smaller teams) to present their individual sales plans.

Restoration — Celebrate last year's success and recognize top performers. Include an element of fun and team building. Do this on the first day because it builds positive energy for the rest of the meeting.

Designing a Day-by-Day Agenda

Allocate two to three days for the kickoff, with each day focused on a different theme with different speakers taking the lead. For example, a three day kickoff could look like this:

Day 1 – Build excitement for the upcoming year with the entire team together, including talks from members of the C-suite (mission and vision content). Get people excited about what is to come. In the evening, schedule a dinner or activity that's local and fun and allows them to build deeper relationships (Restore).

Day 2 – The breakout sessions. This is where the kickoff gets more tactical (with Prepare, Plant, and Tend content). The team works closely with their leaders to take action on the high-level themes discussed during the first day.

Day 3 – Sales reps present business plans that detail how their work in the upcoming year will deliver the results laid out in the plan. It's a great forum for peers to evaluate their teammates and learn from each other. At this point, everyone is tired and preoccupied with going home. Do a brief wrap-up and provide a meal before sending them to the airport.

It's a good balance between fun and work. The team has to digest tons of information supporting the sales plan, and they also spend time with their colleagues from around the country to collaborate, swap ideas, and get excited.

Finally, the sales kickoff should be themed to support the plan or positioning of the plan. It's your job, with the help of your Sales Council, to keep that theme alive and exciting throughout the year. Once you determine the theme for the kickoff, use it as the guiding message for the entire year. Stick with it on your monthly calls and quarterly meetings. Prepare a gift with the year's theme — everybody loves swag.

Here are some questions to consider:

– Is the vision compelling? How well can you articulate the vision?

– Do they understand the importance of their individual contribution to the larger mission?

– Have you demonstrated your expertise? Can you demonstrate, with credibility, how the work needs to be done?

– Do you have enough emotional intelligence to discern if people like you and are willing to do the hard work for you? Think open-door policy: When was the last time someone on your team was vulnerable with you?

– What kind of talent do you need to execute the plan? Do you currently have it on the team? If you don't, do you know where to find the people you need?

– How well does your talent compare to the competition? You need better talent than the competition.

- Who is a good candidate for the Sales Council?

- Have you scheduled your sales kick-off meeting?

Now let's *prepare* the team for success.

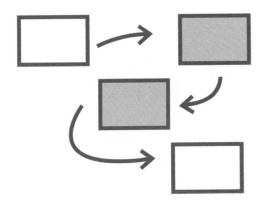

Principle 3

PREPARE

"Chance favors the prepared."

— Louis Pasteur

As the growing season gets underway, the farmer prepares to manage weeds and pests, arranges to rent harvest equipment, books space in a co-op silo or processor. Preparation looks both internally, to the farm, and externally, to partners and suppliers.

The prepared sales leader understands the difference between having a good sales plan and delivering sales results. A good plan, well positioned, with an unprepared sales team is a recipe for a long year, even failure. If you don't know how to prepare your sales team, don't expect to be a sales leader for long. If you are a new sales leader who was recently promoted because you were a top performing rep, then pay close attention.

In order to be prepared for the selling year you must prepare yourself and the team.

Prepare yourself. Build the right team to achieve the plan. How you recruit, hire, and onboard new talent will be critical factors in your success in the selling year. The extent to which you prepare for adversity will help you in good times and bad times. You must believe that the conditions will absolutely, with 100% certainty, turn against you, without warning, at the most inconvenient of times. You'd better be prepared.

Prepare the team. Prepare training for the team and each individual member. You must be able to personalize training and deliver it in a methodical way. Leverage technology so that the team can sell better and faster.

Let's look at both of these tasks in greater detail.

Preparing Yourself

The sales manager is arguably the least-trained employee on the team. How much formal sales management training have you received? Probably very little; effective guidance for sales managers is hard to come by. So you need to train yourself and your managers on their craft.

Building a Team

One of the most important elements of a sales leader's craft is building a team. Your plan for the selling year likely calls for adding reps. Your ability to hit your targets is predicated on having a full sales staff, but it's not enough to just hire more warm bodies. You need to know how to build a best-in-class sales team.

Companies can't build a sales team without great sales leaders, and great sales leaders know how to hire. If you don't hire the right person for the role, then it doesn't matter how well you train them. When a new sales rep fails, it is the company's fault because that person probably shouldn't have been hired.

Hiring is tricky. Hiring salespeople is even trickier. Hiring top-performing salespeople is your hardest task. That's because sales professionals have spent their entire careers interviewing. Think about it: The role of a sales rep is to spend her day being interviewed by prospects and accounts. Reps are professionally trained interviewers. They know what to say and how to say it so that it captures your attention.

Most sales leaders are subjective in their hiring and rely heavily on their own biases. They overemphasize how the interview *felt*. They're easily manipulated by the candidate and don't solicit feedback from other credible sources. They overvalue the résumé, don't properly check references (if they even bother to check references), and, worst of all, hire too many candidates that applied to the job rather than recruiting top sales talent (more on this later).

Hiring the Right Way: Six Steps

Hiring sales professionals is a process with prescribed steps and requires input from multiple stakeholders. This six-step process comes with only one rule: You can't skip a step. Each one is designed to keep you from making a bad hire. Follow the process, and you'll improve your ability to hire top performers.

You're thinking: "I'm in a hurry. I have targets to hit; every day I delay hiring means we're getting deeper in the revenue hole. I need to fill out my team, and fast."

But you know how expensive it is to replace a bad hire. *Forbes* recently published research showing that, on average, it costs around $200,000 to replace a B2B sales rep. Make two bad hires in a year and you're costing your company nearly half a million dollars.

Your responsibility to hire the *right* candidate supersedes any responsibility to hire quickly.

The six steps to hire the ideal salesperson are:

1) Résumé review
2) Human resources (HR) interview
3) Written assessment
4) Video conference interview
5) Personality test
6) Business plan and pitch

While these steps are essential, they don't necessarily need to be taken in this order. While it's preferable to follow this flow so that the hiring team (managers, HR professionals, other stakeholders) knows what to expect, business circumstances may dictate some flexibility.

This six-step screening and selection process is intended to be rigorous and thorough. You've worked hard to create a winning sales culture, and being selective honors your responsibility to preserve the culture. It's not enough to hire talented sales professionals. You must hire the best talent that fits your culture.

Follow this process even for internal or referred candidates. This doesn't mean you can't move quickly: To accelerate the process, shorten the amount of time that lapses between each step.

1.Résumé Review

All candidates must submit a résumé and provide references to human resources (HR). Someone from the HR team will review all new résumés first, looking for the following:

- Numerical examples, quota attainment percentage, and sales rankings
- Clarity on exceptional accomplishments. How did they compare to their peers — for example,

Ranked #1, Rep of the Year, top in product sales, etc. All candidates with sales distinction on their résumés will be sent to the sales manager for review.

That said … Most résumés simply tell you what the applicant's roles and responsibilities were in previous jobs. You may occasionally see a strong résumé that also tells you what the candidate accomplished that his peers didn't. A good résumé doesn't read like this: *Managed the largest territory for the genetics division.* It reads like this: *Grew sales by 135% in assigned genetics accounts from 2017-2019,* or *Voted 2019 Sales Professional of the Year for best sales results on the team.*

Yes, the sales candidate's résumé is important. It should help her secure the interview. But it shouldn't be the sole input in your hiring decision. Just like closing a new account is a process, so is identifying, selecting, and hiring top-performing sales talent.

The decision to move a candidate forward is yours, but you need to provide feedback to HR quickly, ideally within 24 hours.

2. The 30-Minute HR Interview

HR starts the hiring process with a quick get-to-know-you initial phone screen. This step should be conducted by a member of the HR team, with you on the line mainly to listen, ask a few questions, and share the benefits of working with the company. It's a great way to weed out the crazies and sniff out the winners. During the call, ask yourself two simple questions: "Do I like this person? Will he represent our company well to our market?" If not, don't waste your time. Keep looking.

3. Written Assessment

The goal of the written assessment is to get a glimpse at how a candidate thinks and how he expresses those thoughts (can he think and write clearly?). Writing is

a window to the mind. Forward a set of questions to the candidate and ask that he respond directly to you within 48 hours.
Here are some sample questions:

1. Why do you want to work with us?
2. What is the most generous thing your current company or a previous employer has done for you?
3. What is the most outside-the-box idea you have had in your professional career? What were the results?
4. Of all the accomplishments of your career, which is the one that makes you stand out? Why?
5. Tell me about a time when you were in over your head on a project. How did you handle it?
6. What is the most important professional goal you have yet to achieve?
7. What keeps you up at night, and what do you do to relieve stress?
8. What is something about you that people would be surprised to learn?
9. What makes an effective sales manager? What is the one trait that often derails their career?
10. If you had a boat, what would you name it?

 ## 4. Video Conference Interview

The video conference interview is conducted by the sales manager. It's the part of the interview process where you'll learn the most about a candidate. The interview is one hour in length and broken down into four sections:

1. Rapid-fire Q&A (10 minutes)
2. Interview questions (30 minutes)
3. Presentation of the role (10 minutes)
4. Candidate questions (10 minutes)

The main objective of this interview is to see how the candidate handles discomfort. Up to this point, most of the interview process has felt normal to the candidate. This conversation should feel anything but normal. The candidate should feel uncomfortable, because selling is an uncomfortable job. For the first 40 minutes of this hour-long conversation, you'll ask hard questions that should provoke discomfort. If the candidate can maintain composure, then you've got a strong potential hire. Second to résumé review, this step eliminates more candidates than the other steps combined.

Other objectives of this interview are to determine if the candidate is presentable, makes the audience comfortable, is engaging and asks questions, is conversational, is interested and interesting, and is skilled at softly closing by asking to continue the conversation with your company.

5. Personality Test

So many personality tests are available in the market, and many are free. Understanding a candidate's personality is critical to understanding how to lead them. You need to know how your individual team members think, process feedback, view the world, and most important, prefer to be coached. The personality tool you use is less important than accurately interpreting the results.

6. Business Plan and Pitch

This meeting is the final stage of the interview process and should be conducted at the corporate offices. All candidates should work with the sales manager to prepare and distribute a presentation file 24 hours before the interview. The objectives of the presentation-style interview is to determine if the candidate: understands the market, knows how to identify potential referral sources, understands the competitive landscape, and can effectively pitch the company (communicating company differentiators and value propositions).

This is also an opportunity to gauge a candidate's comfort level with technology and ability to command a room. Other members of the executive team are encouraged to attend this interview and provide the sales manager with feedback on the candidate.

Would all of your existing sales reps pass this process? Perhaps not. But the reason that you're investing in a formal hiring game plan is because you've identified an opportunity to increase the effectiveness of your team.

Is this too rigorous? Absolutely. It will deter some candidates. And that's the point. It will weed out lots of prospective employees — but not the good ones. The top performers will shine under the pressure.

Going Beyond the Résumé: The 3 Cs

If you've ever hired salespeople, you know that no two interviews are alike. The objective is to find talent with both tangible and intangible characteristics that will easily segue into a role at your company. Every candidate has a different story, expectation, and array of skills, and the quicker that salesperson becomes productive, the better the situation is for everyone. As the sales leader, it's your job to ask the right sequence of questions during the interview in order to understand what drives this person, how she operates in a professional setting, and how she responds to challenges, all of which are strong indicators for success in a selling role.

> **The ideal candidate will have the willingness, intelligence, passion, and skills necessary to develop a successful sales career under your coaching.**

How do you pull these characteristics out of the candidate during the interview process? It's a difficult task. Three attributes are most important in the ideal salesperson: *character*, *chemistry*, and *competence*. These three characteristics can be assessed in an interview by asking the right questions and closely listening to the responses the candidate gives.

Character

You want to hire a salesperson who isn't afraid to be real — a person you can trust to get the job done and who holds himself accountable when he messes up. In order to evaluate a candidate's character, you need to know where he is coming from, how he arrived where he is, and where he sees himself ending up. An indicator of strong character is when you hear a candidate confidently talk about mistakes he's made and what he learned from them. If you ask a candidate, "What's your biggest weakness?" and he provides a response that resembles, "I work too much" or "I'm too competitive," then the interview is over. Those aren't real weaknesses. Seek responses like, "I struggle to manage conflict" or "I tend to wait until the last minute to finish my reports." These are real opportunities to improve.

> **An indicator of strong character is when a candidate confidently talks about mistakes he's made and what he learned from them.**

Chemistry

Next up is chemistry. Looking for chemistry highlights the importance of compatibility — to work with a team, the candidate needs to mesh in his relationships, habits, goals, and work ethic. You aren't looking for someone who just wants another job. The best salesperson will care about what he is selling, who he is working with, and how he gets it all done. Discovering chemistry with a candidate can provide valuable insight that can prove beneficial to the organization and goes beyond basic qualifications and/or typical answers to standard interview questions. For example, I like to ask a candidate the last book they read. If they can't remember, then we aren't going to work well together. I'm not judging them for not being a reader, but rather observing that I believe leaders are readers, and I'm looking for leaders. (See more on the value of reading in the Restore principle.)

> **Discovering chemistry with a candidate can provide valuable insight that can prove beneficial to the organization and goes beyond their basic qualifications and typical answers to standard interview questions.**

Competence

Competence is the attribute most hiring managers look for first, but it ranks last among the Three Cs. While your best candidate will impress you with what she initiates on her own and how she takes responsibility for her own professional growth, it doesn't mean that she has to know everything right out of the gate. If she possesses a solid character and shares great chemistry with you and the team, then competence is something you can teach her.

> **The right talent will train themselves — they will put in the long nights studying or on the phone with other team members until they master their craft.**

Yes, you're understandably motivated to hire quickly; not having a full team makes it difficult to reach your growth goals. But making a bad hire can be a costly mistake. Remember the saying: "Slow to hire, quick to fire."

Extending an Offer

All offers should include a 90-day probationary period. The offer letter should clearly detail the activity and results expected of the candidate in the first 90 days on the job. It should also state that permanent employment is contingent upon the results of the 90 day review. (You will learn how to properly conduct a sales rep's 90-day review in the Performance Appraisal appendix.)

Preparing for Adversity

Even when your team is firing on all cylinders, consistently delivering great sales results, you must constantly believe that the conditions will absolutely, with 100% certainty, turn against you, without warning, at the most inconvenient of times. You'd better be prepared.

By embracing the unending possibilities of danger that can affect your performance, you will put yourself in a superior position to hit your targets. In Jim Collin's Book *Great by Choice*, he refers to preparing for adversity as "productive paranoia." He writes, "Paranoid behavior is enormously functional *if* fear is channeled into extensive preparation and calm, clear-headed action."

Preparing for adversity isn't just about anticipating threats to your team's success; it's also about the mission and vision of the company. It's worrying about protecting the team and culture you and the leadership group have established, and building something bigger than this year's sales targets. Expect adversity. Expect surprises to surface when everything seems to be going well.

Here's a short list of factors that can derail a sales team on target:

1. **Running too hard.** Sports coaches love to say, "We can't be undefeated if we don't win the first game." Many sales managers take this same approach. They focus hard on hitting the first month's number, overextending the team in the process. Early success feels great, but it can cost a sales team too. Nothing fails like success. Too much exertion in Month 1 leads to a hangover in Month 2.

2. **Weather delays.** Many sales leaders fail to account for weather and actually lose a few more selling days because of road conditions, cancelled flights, and cancelled school (when customers and salespeople who can't find childcare must stay home with kids). Just because you live in San Diego doesn't mean your customers do too.

3. **Unexpected departures.** Good people leave good teams for circumstances unrelated to the job and company. There's no way to anticipate when this will happen, but you'd better plan for it. Your top rep might go on maternity leave and not return, move to a different city so that a spouse could pursue a different career opportunity, or decide to stay home and attend to an ailing parent. Sadly, I've had to lead a team through the tragic death of a teammate who left the earth way too soon.

4. **Failed forecasting.** For some reason, sales executives always budget for the next month to be better than the previous month. Maybe it's pressure from leadership and investors, maybe it's inexperience with forecasting. Either way, it's the same result: a big miss. There hasn't been a sales team that wasn't affected by seasonality in some way. It's great to be aggressive and push the team to produce. However, sales leaders can compromise their credibility among colleagues when they publish a silly hockey-stick forecast that doesn't account for the nuances of the business.

Here's how you plan for unexpected adversity:

Back off the budget in challenging months. Let's say you've met your sales number for January, so your year's off to a good start and you're building credibility with leadership and the sales team. Look back at last February and make sure this year is better than last, but don't be too aggressive. Consider the facts and publish an accurate forecast based on the realities of this short month. Other seasonal issues to consider:

- Is it realistic for your business to have its biggest month of sales in December?
- Does summer vacation affect sales?

Create "snow days." Have each rep create and share an alternate plan for those unexpected weather events. A good "snow day" plan is full of activities we always plan for, but that keep getting pushed further down the task list. These include: prospecting blitzes, writing an annual sales plan (that they were supposed to write in December or January but never did), taking an online course, reading a book that improves their craft, practicing pitches and presentations with other sales team members, and any other nonrevenue-producing activity.

TDY. The military has a beautiful concept called temporary duty (TDY). It can also be a gift for a sales manager. In fact, this seldom-used tactic can make you look like a hero to your executive team. If you anticipate a major storm in a market that will sideline a sales rep, then temporarily send them to another market. If it's a senior rep that is going to be hit with inclement weather, then send them to cross-train on a different product or to help train a more junior salesperson. If it's a junior salesperson, then send them to work with a top performer in another market.

Here's an additional benefit of this tactic: variety is motivating. Many salespeople rarely leave their markets. A TDY can mix things up for a rep, give them a little "sunshine" or a chance to connect with teammates they rarely speak with, and they always return energized and grateful for the experience.

Preparing the Team

Training: Structured & Ongoing

Training is something you do — always, at every level of the sales organization, including you. Not just the first week for new reps. Not just for the 90-day probationary period. Always. Training fails many sales teams because it's only reserved for the newest or underperforming members.

True professionals always train. Surely you've encountered that all-star rep who's always reading a business book or sharing interesting articles with you. You know, the one who consistently hits target, but acts like she's on a performance improvement plan? There's a reason why she stays at the top of the sales rankings, and it's because she's always learning.

1. Create a Training Plan for Everyone

Training must be structured. And every team member, not just new and underperforming reps, should have a professional development plan. That means having a defined curriculum that's tailored to the unique needs of each person on the team. Everyone's development plan should be different. You will see some overlap between reps in areas that need training, but the more you can customize it, the better.

Here are some key elements that should exist in a thorough training plan:

- Product
- Craft
- Industry changes
- Competition
- Company

Product. This is straightforward, yet many sales leaders only provide product training to new reps and when launching a new product. You must constantly train everyone on product because people forget information over time, and your product is always changing.

Craft. You must always train on your craft: selling. NFL quarterbacks don't stop training their throwing arm because they've been playing football forever. Tenured sales reps still need to train on selling. If we only train on product enhancements or changes to the corporate structure, then we are failing our team. Regularly scheduled training on skills related to selling is a must: prospecting, account management, overcoming client resistance, etc.

Don't forget to train yourself and other sales managers on their craft. A leader's craft is different; it includes: recruiting, hiring, onboarding, managing a budget, leadership, etc.

Industry changes. Your industry is constantly changing. Keep your team abreast so that you aren't surprised by seismic shifts that could affect your performance.

Competition. You should know your competition like you know your own company. It's that simple.

Company. To most customers, your team is the face and voice of the company. When the company makes a change, your team has to be the first to know. There's nothing more frustrating for a rep than to hear about changes in the company from a customer or, worse, a competitor.

2. Structure Your Training Program

When sales professionals fail, it's the manager's fault. You must audit your team's current training process and make sure the training is thorough and effective so that the team is prepared for success. Be proactive in making it easier for your team to do their jobs by arming them with insight.

Schedule training at least once a month, ideally weekly. Shorter duration at a higher frequency works best. You should have a defined and published training curriculum. You need a new hire training program, a new manager training program, and a schedule for ongoing training that everyone attends.

3. Teach the new reps.

For most companies, sales training simply consists of sending newly hired reps to shadow a top performing rep in the company. This system is not only terribly disruptive to your top performers, who have to sideline their usual work, but a typical day for a top performer is drastically different from what a new rep will experience.

If you want to build a sales team that consistently produces superior results, then you have to deliver a consistent, scalable, and repeatable sales training product. The first 30 days of a rep's career are the most important. And guess what? He won't close a single deal in that first month. The first month should be focused on learning. This focus is guided by a training program that utilizes self-paced home study, workshops, peer mentorship, field rides, and shadow sessions.

Here's what that agenda looks like:

Week 1 (Self-Paced Pre-Work & Team Huddles)	Company & Culture	Products	Competitive	Customer Stories	Certification Prep
	Mentorship (One-on-ones with team & daily check-ins)				
Week 2 (Boot Camp Workshop)	Travel Day	Executive Welcome Worshop & Networking	Case Study Team Exercise	Case Study / Sales Process / Certification Prep	Prep Work / Pitch Certification
Week 3 (Field Readiness)	Team Building Evening Events				Territory Planning & Readiness Certification
	Compelling Events	Social Prospecting	Prospecting Outreach	Discovery Questions	
	Mentorship (One-on-ones with team)				
Week 4 (Building Pipeline & Closing Business)	Self-paced	Certification	Workshop	Mentorship	Pipeline & Deal Review
	Sales Process (Daily Check-ins)				

Your training calendar should reflect the essential learning areas of your program. (If, as you're reading this, you realize that your company's sales training is weak, then read *SalesHood* by Elay Cohen.)

Intangibles of a Training Program

Regardless of industry or offering, there are some universal truths about sales training that you should adopt. It should be built around the most important skills and learning goals a rep needs in order to succeed in the company. Here are the five areas to focus on:

1. Culture

Every team has a unique culture; it will make or break your team. Of the five critical components of sales training, this is the most important. Yet most companies have no control of the culture the team has created and therefore don't focus on culture in training. When you include culture in training you set a standard for how things get done on your team. It sets a precedent that *how* you succeed is more important than *what* you accomplished. A healthy culture will unify your team and teach them how to leverage the strengths of each member.

2. Product

Product training is a critical part of a comprehensive training program. All competitive training, including objection handling, should be covered in product training. However, while understanding your product and solution is a critical part of sales training, most companies spend too much time focusing solely on product training. It's paramount, but it should not be your only focus. It's important to find a balance.

3. Process

Take time to do a deep dive on your sales process in order to teach reps how to move prospects to buyers in a linear, step-by-step process. Be specific. Share stories of real customers and how reps were able to successfully close deals. Once training is over and your reps begin their day-to-day work, they'll naturally tend to resort back to the habits and routines they've used before. Providing solid training on your sales process overrides that habit and lets them focus on the new skills they've obtained.

4. Skills

Ongoing skills development is a sign of a healthy sales culture. When this is done right, managers regularly schedule time with reps to review opportunities for improvement, from prospecting and pipeline management, to negotiating and pitching. Sales skills should always be a focus of the training. Even if you hire professionally trained sales associates, get in the habit of routinely practicing sales skills to ensure they stay sharp and up to date.

5. Scheduling

The last thing you want is a rep who isn't sure how to design her day. It's important that reps walk away from training with a personal schedule and a clear understanding of what tasks need to be accomplished with deadlines for each. As a manager, you expect accurate and timely reporting in addition to setting activity expectations. So make sure they know how and when to complete the critical tasks, such as submitting a forecast, drafting account plans, logging sales activities, and submitting quotes and orders.

Leveraging Technology to Sell Better & Faster

"Recognize that it is far better to find a few smart people and give them the best technology than to have a great number of people who are less equipped." — Ray Dalio, Principles

Technology will be very important in your approach to the Plant principle and the Tend principle.

Over the past decade, the sales industry has experienced technological advancements that forever changed the frontline sales position. In the early 2000s, customer relationship management (CRM) software was only helpful for managers and executives to manage forecasts and activities. Ten years ago, the CRM only created administrative work for sales reps. It took them out of the field and kept them off the phone. The best reps were forced to sacrifice nights and weekends to enter data so that they could keep their selling hours during the week. It was a painful time to be a sales rep. The technology was so ineffective that many reps refused to use it. It drove managers crazy and has become a great source of humor for today's sales memes.

Good news is that CRMs have come a long way. But this principle isn't about the CRM. It's about new technology that supplements the CRM, making it easier for sales teams to sell faster and better. You must prepare your sales team to leverage modern selling technology to 1) accelerate your current sales process and eliminate administratively burdensome and expensive nonselling tasks for salespeople, and 2) retain more accounts and create a better buying experience by giving the sales team all the material they need with just a click on their device.

Accelerating Pipeline

If you can't measure it, then you can't improve it. You likely have a metric or two in your business that is painfully administrative to measure, yet profoundly important to the success of the business. So you have people track it manually and report on the metrics at some frequency (probably not frequently enough). Too often, key pipeline metrics like stage-by-stage conversion or win-loss ratios are subjected to this practice, and because you haven't yet automated the generation and reporting of pipeline data, you can't immediately see what's slowing down your sales.

If you want to accelerate the pipeline and see exactly how fast deals can move from brand new to closed, then make sure you have automatic tracking and reporting for your key metrics. Your CRM is only as good as the data that exists within it. No brainer, right? But how much important data exists outside of the CRM? Many sales teams have disparate data management systems, and it drives sales leaders crazy because they don't have a true picture of their sales pipeline when they look at the CRM. Sometimes you even make bad decisions because you aren't looking at all of the data. It's like driving with one eye closed. Here are some common examples:

Call tracking is in the phone system, so the CRM can't tell you how many calls you received yesterday, how many were answered, and how that compared to previous periods.

Traffic and conversion metrics are siloed in Google analytics, your marketing automation platform, or a similar tool, so tracking how many new leads were created isn't available in the CRM.

Other conversion elements exist in another tool. For example, many of my healthcare clients track patient leads, admissions into clinical services, and other key metrics in an electronic health record (EHR) system, which is separate from the CRM.

Financial data that helps a sales leader know revenue potential by stage is often in a separate quoting system.

Gaining visibility to all data is the only way to accelerate your sales pipeline. For example, imagine that you are behind on "closed/won" business for the month. The CRM shows that you have plenty of opportunities that should close by the end of the month, but all the opportunity-specific data exists outside the CRM. You don't know how long it takes for a viable opportunity to close or what's needed from whom to progress the opportunity to closed. The CRM only shows you how many aggregate opportunities there are by stage (and date created, if you're lucky). What's missing is an alarm bell that alerts you to opportunities that have languished in a particular stage for too long. (This is called a "rotting report," and we will cover it and others in the Tend principle.)

As you prepare for the selling year, you must make sure you and the sales team gain access to all the data they need, in real time, to accelerate the pipeline. Without real-time access to key pipeline data points, your forecasts are guesses at best.

Think about your sales pipeline: What are all the metrics you need to track so that you have the complete picture? Here are a few examples to help you get started:

- Total leads created by date, source, and type
- Total calls (inbound and outbound), calls answered, call length, call source
- Average cycle time from newly created lead to closed/won or lost
- Time at each stage of your sales funnel

Every stage of your sales funnel needs to be managed independently and meticulously in real time. Knowing these data points allow you to benchmark performance, measure performance for the metrics, and intervene quickly so that you can better manage your sales velocity.

The technology exists to aggregate all your relevant sales data into one consolidated dashboard that can be accessed in real time from any device, anywhere. It's up to you to work with your data analytics or IT team to make pipeline metrics important and visible.

Customer Success and Retention

It's far easier and cheaper to keep an account than it is to create a new one. Technology designed to help sales teams stay top of mind for your accounts is affordable and easily accessible. Investing in customer success and retention technology is required in today's marketplace.

Whether it's automating the onboarding experience for new accounts or making existing accounts aware of a new offering, there's a piece of technology for you.

You should also use technology to enhance your account onboarding experience and to ensure your accounts are always aware of everything your sales team can do for them. Think about the ideal onboarding experience for a new account. What points of communication are standard and can be automatically conducted without a human? How well do you use technology to keep customers informed of company or product updates? Does technology let you and the account know when they have a need for one of your products or services? Or do you rely solely on a sales rep to uncover opportunities to upsell and cross-sell within existing accounts?

What could be possible for your sales team and accounts if you let technology automate some of the necessary but administratively burdensome tasks of your sales process? Aside from freeing up more time for your reps to sell, you can also expect to sell more to your existing accounts while improving overall account satisfaction.

The tools are cheap in comparison to your current workflow. It's expensive to waste talented people's time doing low-impact administrative tasks that could be automated. It's *really* expensive to lose customers because you haven't streamlined the necessary touchpoints of onboarding and account retention. As you prepare for the upcoming sales year, identify the ways technology can help you lead more effectively and help your team sell better and faster.

For Executives Considering Hiring a VP of Sales

This section is specifically written for CEOs and investors who are considering hiring a Vice President of Sales. If you are approaching a selling year and wondering if you need a VP of Sales, then keep reading.

Unfortunately, too many sales organizations make the mistake of hiring a VP too early.

The VP of Sales is a huge role within a company, yet the title has been used in such a broad context that we have diluted the actual role of what the individual actually does. The VP of Sales is responsible for the executive function of a company's revenue generation. She is responsible for recruiting, hiring, training, and leading the sales team; creating and communicating sales goals; and leading the unit that generates most (or all) of the business for the company. She must be able to clearly map the customer's journey from first contact to post-purchase, create specialization within the roles of a sales force, and define territories and strategy for new markets. But very few VPs are actually VPs.

Companies in the early stages of launching are most likely to get this wrong. If you are a new company or startup and you don't have sales reps or managers on board before hiring your VP of Sales, then you've made a huge mistake. Hold off on hiring a VP of Sales until you are ready to start, scale, and build a sales team — not just to start your company's selling efforts.

Before you hire your next VP of Sales, take a moment to decide if your company needs this role, and if so, how it should be filled. Don't hire a VP of sales until it's time to fund and grow a sales team.

If you are an early-stage company, your first sales hire should never be a VP; it should always be a sales rep — a very good sales rep. While a VP may make you look good to the board, what an early stage company really needs is a Super Rep. A Super Rep is the person who can be the No. 1 advocate for your company, who begins bringing in revenue, and who goes out and simply sells, sells, and sells some more. In contrast, a good VP of Sales should only spend about 10% of his time selling; the other 90% is spent strategizing, coaching, and managing.

On the other end of the spectrum, well-established companies can miss badly on their VP of Sales hires too. Once you've established your company and are ready to hire (or change) a VP of Sales, the error stems from promoting one of your top reps or managers into the role. This ends up being a mistake because often the VP spends too much of his time directly selling and working with customers and not enough time building training programs, strategizing new product offerings, coaching reps on maximizing sales, pondering joint ventures, managing board and executive team expectations, and leading his sales force.

Without the VP of Sales performing VP of Sales work, a company's sales system breaks down. The VP may think he's doing the right thing. Rather, the company has put the wrong person in the wrong role by promoting a rep or manager. It is worth going outside of the company and hiring the right person for the VP of Sales in order to ensure the role is filled correctly and the company's needs for that role are met.

The Vice President of Sales is a role that can make or break a company, which is why it's crucial to find the right person to fill the position. It's not the first hire in the sales organization, and she probably doesn't work for your company today.

Here are some questions to consider:

- Do each of your direct reports have a personalized development plan for the upcoming year?

- Have you defined a hiring process? Have you published the plan to the team and to human resources? If you need outsourced recruiting, have you secured it?

- Do you have a defined sales training playbook for all new hires?

- Where in your sales team will you adopt new technology so that your team will be more effective?

Moving From Strategy to Sowing

You've built a good sales plan, positioned the team to march, and prepared the team for success. In the next principles, we will discuss executing the plan. The first principle on execution is Planting.

Planting is 1) creating new harvest opportunities for the selling year. and 2) moving resources (including people) into the field so that they can grow during the selling year.

The strategy work is finished. Now let's get out in the field and *plant.*

Principle 4
PLANT

"Don't judge each day by the harvest you reap but by the seeds that you plant."
— Robert Louis Stevenson

Ask any farmer and he will tell you that without planting, there's nothing to harvest. Sounds self-explanatory. Yet if we look at the principle through the lens of a sales leader, you would probably agree that most sales teams spend too much time on closing (harvesting) and not enough time on prospecting (planting). Whether you lead a sales team for a growing company that needs more customers or your company has a more established account base, planting will make or break your selling year.

Successful sales teams go into each new selling year knowing what they need to plant. When you assess your team, it's likely you need to plant new accounts and you need to plant within your existing accounts. Everyone on the sales team, including you and some key executives (C-suite), has planting responsibilities.

This book won't teach you any new prospecting tactics, because those books already exist. (If you want to learn more about the practice of prospecting, then read Marylou Tyler's work *Predictable Revenue* and

Predictable Prospecting.) This principle is meant to teach you how to build prospecting responsibilities into every role on the sales team.

When Sales Teams Stop Planting

At some point in your career, you will lead a team that has stopped planting. They get caught up managing existing accounts, ensuring that they keep the business. It's a dangerous position, and it can stealthily and quickly derail a selling year. It's your responsibility to intervene. At some point, every account will leave you, but it's hard to know when. Sometimes there's no warning. And it never happens at a convenient time.

You're not planting enough if your sales team is responsible for every stage of your sales funnel.

If *all* of your reps are required to:

– Enter new prospects into the CRM
– Make calls and send emails to these prospects in hopes that they have a need for your offering
– Convert a percentage of these prospects into new accounts
– Maintain a list of active accounts
– Sell all of your offerings to their assigned accounts
– Service a select few accounts that make up a disproportionately large amount of your revenue

then you are in a vulnerable position.

Sales reps are smart: They follow the money. Most of their income is tied to sales, so they spend all of their time on existing accounts. By this logic, prospecting gets neglected or abandoned. What makes this problem hard for you to identify is that most of your reps are meeting or exceeding their sales targets. In the Prepare principle, you learned to prepare for adversity. Adversity might be losing a top account or a top rep. Sometimes it's even worse: A top rep leaves and takes *all* of her accounts with her. If you haven't focused enough attention on planting, you'll have a big hole to fill and hitting your targets might be impossible. Guess what? The board of directors doesn't care. They still expect you to hit plan. So what's the solution?

Redefining Your Team: Generalists Versus Specialists

In 2014, I was leading a sales team that had just had its best year ever for the company. We hit our revenue targets and the reps were earning more money than they ever imagined. Even with a growth target of 40% more sales than the previous year, I felt like we had enough accounts to achieve our sales targets. We had assigned the growth to the accounts, as we discussed in the Plan principle. Each rep had a good strategy for his existing accounts, which we will cover in great detail in the Tend principle. Then I read Marylou Tyler's book *Predictable Revenue.*

I realized that my team was responsible for every stage of our sales funnel. Every rep had a healthy number of assigned accounts and would stay plenty busy harvesting sales throughout the year. But what would happen when adversity reared its ugly head? It didn't make sense to refocus my team away from existing business to generating new business. Tyler's book taught me to create specialization on the team.

I created a team of sales development reps (SDRs) to focus solely on identifying and developing new accounts. The result? We tripled the number of active accounts in a single year, without disrupting our existing business.

If you have a sales team of more than 10 reps, then it's time to shift from generalists to specialists.

Specialization can take many forms. Sometimes it involves creating a specialty sales unit to sell a unique product. Other times it looks like creating specialized teams based on deal size. The bigger the team gets and the more accounts you have, the more you need to specialize. You might wind up with three or four different sales teams that all report to you.

Where do you start specializing? Create one team (SDRs) focused on planting for new accounts and another team (account managers) focused on maintaining and growing existing accounts. The SDRs only work at the top of your sales funnel, converting prospects into new accounts. They never prospect within existing accounts; that's the job of the assigned account manager.

Start by hiring two people to this top-of-funnel team, not one. You'll learn more, faster, by letting them work alongside one another. If you hire just one SDR, then you don't know if it's working or not working because of the person or the process. Plus, it's good for them to have a healthy sense of competition with each other. They need to work together, in an office; rarely does this position work well in a remote situation. SDRs need a dedicated, quiet space. They also need adequate technology (we'll cover that later).

When the SDR team creates a new account, they get rewarded, and the account then gets assigned to an account manager. Two core benefits of this model:

1. The SDR team quickly gets back to finding new account
2. The account managers are better at managing existing business than a SDR.

Make this shift and watch your accounts growth skyrocket.

You'll need to do a few things for the SDR team to be successful.

1) Create Ideal Account Profiles

Work with your account managers to clearly define the perfect account. Use these questions to create four or five different account profiles, and share them with the team so that your SDRs know where to focus their prospecting efforts.

- How big is the company?
- Where is the company located?
- What industry does the company operate in?
- What problem(s) do they have that we can solve?
- What are the titles of people within the organization that are likely to need our offerings?

2) Find Your Ideal Accounts

Finding new accounts is easier than it's ever been. Start with LinkedIn. It's a great resource. Where does your ideal customer hang out? What information do they consume? Here's a short list:

- Conferences
- Trade publications
- Products and services used in conjunction with your offering
- Networking groups and forums

Don't buy customer lists; that's a lazy and tired tactic. Lists are great, but they need to be used carefully and respectfully. Use them carefully because many lists have bad information. In many instances the names and titles are outdated, and the contact information is wrong, missing, or incomplete. Use them respectfully because often the contacts on the list are unaware that their information has been sold or distributed to you. They aren't expecting your outreach, and sometimes aren't excited to hear from your sales team.

Instead of buying prospect lists, build a strong relationship with your marketing department.

Working With Marketing

Most sales and marketing teams operate in silos — or worse, as adversaries. It's dysfunctional and stagnates growth. This is because the lines between sales and marketing have never been blurrier. The SDR team should help improve your partnership with marketing because both functions are focused on accounts that likely don't know your company exists.

Schedule a meeting with your marketing team and show them your Planting plan. Show them (with data) why separating this function from account management makes good sense. Show them your ideal account profiles. Ask them to critique your plan and provide suggestions. Most marketing teams don't realize how good they are at prospecting. Worse, most sales leaders don't know how good marketers can be at prospecting. Chances are the marketing team has tools, reports, and other assets to help you bolster your SDR team.

If you really want to improve your partnership with marketing and give your SDR team a great chance at being successful, ask if they can physically locate in the marketing department. By osmosis, they will know more about how the company is being positioned to the market, they will better understand the competitive landscape, and, most important, they will learn about every asset (landing pages, print collaterals, webinars, product info, upcoming events, etc.) that the marketing team is deploying to attract new customers.

Leveraging Technology

Now that you have marketing on your side, it's time to provide your SDR team with the tech stack (the hardware and software) to accelerate the pace of account acquisition. The tools they need are specific to their roles and different from the technology that account managers use. In the sales community, this area of focus is generally referred to as *sales enablement*.

Let's start with an outbound prospecting and nurturing software. This type of software typically bolts onto your existing customer relationship management system (CRM), the software, discussed in the previous principle, that you currently use to manage accounts and prospects. Software for the SDR team provides a seamless experience for both of your selling teams. It automates outbound activity like calls, texts, emails, and social media interactions, saving time and reducing workload while logging everything in the CRM.

If you don't currently have a tool like this, then you can easily find one. I've used Outreach.io, SalesLoft, and Apollo.io, and there are countless others ranging in price and sophistication. Your existing CRM may well have this capability. If not, ask marketing if they have a tool that could work. You might be surprised to learn that this tool has been under your nose all along.

It's worth considering hiring a consultant who specializes in top-of-funnel work, especially if most of this is new to you. Setting up an SDR team is important, so invest in getting it right so that you look like a magician to your executive team. A consultant will help you pick the right software, work with marketing to ensure you have the right sales collateral, identity prospects that meet the ideal account profile, and most important, establish some performance benchmarks.

Keep track of all the expenses associated with setting up a specialized SDR group: people, creative needs, technology, and consultants. You should be able to break even in 90 to 120 days. Break even means that you've created enough new accounts with a cumulative transaction value larger than the expenses required to acquire them.

Everyone Still Plants

When you create specialized teams, expect your current team (who now serve as account managers) to be relieved on the one hand and resistant on the other. They will *believe* that their days of prospecting are over, but that couldn't be further from the truth.

Why They Are Relieved

Every time a rep goes to a meeting with a prospect that doesn't have much potential, that's lost time that could have been better spent on deepening their relationships with top accounts. Some of your reps can't spend much time developing new customers because their existing business requires a high level of service. The new SDR team will relieve them of that prospecting work — so they'll thank you.

But here's the catch: Just because the account managers no longer own most of the company's new account creation doesn't mean they no longer have a responsibility to plant. Account managers know which prospects could fundamentally change their business and yours. Account managers are probably your best reps and give the company the best shot at closing these accounts. So keep the prospecting responsibilities of 20-50 big accounts in the hands of your account managers. Hold them accountable for closing a few big accounts each year.

Remind your account managers of their responsibility to plant within their existing account base. Make sure the team is uncovering new buyers within their assigned accounts. They must also make sure all existing offerings are being used, when appropriate. The goal of separating new account prospecting from your account managers is to free them up to saturate *all* your offerings into *all* assigned accounts.

Why They Are Resistant

Eventually the account managers will complain about the SDR team. Predictably, their gripes will include:

- The new accounts aren't *really* qualified.
- The account manager would have handled a situation differently.

  – The SDR team is stepping on their toes or creating
    confusion for customers.

All of these potential scenarios (and there are more) are just signs
of growth. They are normal and healthy problems you will work
through with the team. Anticipate these challenges, prepare your
team to address them, and remind them of why we are doing it
(mission, vision, plan). Invite the team to come up with ideas to help
seamlessly transition business from the SDR team to the account
management team.

Everyone Plants — Including You

As the leader, you have a unique position to win and keep business
that your reps can't replicate. You bring a unique perspective — and a
fancy title. Think back to your selling career. You can easily think of a
situation where bringing in a "big title" to a meeting was a huge win.

Are you doing enough of this for your team?

When was the last time you helped a rep close a big account?

It's *your job* to know when you, the CEO, or another key executive
needs to be brought in on an opportunity. Don't place this responsibility
on the reps. As you conduct your monthly account review briefings,
discuss how you or another executive can help plant. (If you want to
learn more about account reviews, it's covered in the Tend principle.)

Each week, you need to spend time working opportunities that
only you can influence. These opportunities could be large accounts,
strategic partnerships, or joint ventures.

Recruiting Is Planting

We covered recruiting extensively in the Prepare principle. But
it's worth covering here because you are the only person who is
responsible for identifying and recruiting your next best sales talent.

You may not have any openings on your sales team, but that could change tomorrow. Better to have a pipeline of talent ready to come work for you than to leave a territory vacant because you didn't anticipate a rep leaving.

LinkedIn is the easiest tool for this type of planting. You can run and save searches based on keywords. Connect with sales talent and ask them to tell you more about what they do. You aren't necessarily interviewing them, but you're proactively keeping your candidate pipeline full. Make this part of your weekly schedule. Don't wait for openings before you start planting people.

Plant Early

Your sales plan likely called for more reps to be hired, so start planting your recruiting seeds now. If you don't get your new hires planted early enough in the selling year for them to grow, learn, and mature, then they have no chance of ramping up fast enough to contribute to targets. If you leave positions open for six months into the selling year, they'll miss their sales targets. Unlike farming, there's no significant penalty for a sales leader planting new reps early. There's no late-season freeze in selling, only adequate time to develop.

You're doing your job well when you already have a list of people you will hire next, months in advance of actually needing them.

Emphasize Quality Over Quantity

In farming and selling, quality always matters more than quantity. If the seed is of poor quality, it doesn't matter how much you plant. Don't expect much hay in the barn.

Remember this truth as you develop new accounts, plant new reps, and manage selling activity. You only need a handful of really special accounts to fundamentally change your business. Each new rep should have a shot at becoming your next best rep, or don't hire them.

Finally, focus on the activity that actually drives business. Don't run your team ragged chasing activity metrics that you know have little to no impact on a sales rep's success. Yes, there's no substitute for *the right activity*. Too much focus on activity for its own sake will prompt your reps into gaming the system, and you'll be left with a false sense of progress. You'd rather have a rep conducting 20 great meetings each week with highly qualified accounts than taking 30 meetings just to tell you he had 30 meetings. Enforce quality.

Here are some questions to consider:

- Have you created ideal account profiles for your company? Do the profiles vary by offering?

- How will you and the team better collaborate with marketing this year? How's your relationship with the marketing leader? How can you make it better this year?

- Does everyone on the team understand their individual responsibility to plant seeds? Is it clear that everyone will prospect in the next year? – How will you measure new opportunities by rep?

The judgement of a sales leader is determined by the harvest. Harvests come months after planting, but just because you've planted doesn't guarantee a harvest. How you tend to your work between planting and harvesting is what counts. Let's learn how to ***tend.***

Principle 5

TEND

"Things do not happen. Things are made to happen."
— John F. Kennedy

Tending the crops after planting creates favorable conditions that stimulate healthy, vigorous growth and robust production. Tending also keeps the crops from being suppressed by weeds and protects them from other potential sources of harm such as animals, insects, and disease.

Tending your sales revenue is essentially the same practice. Re-read the paragraph above, but replace the word crop with account, opportunity, or revenue. Also recognize that weeds, animals, insects, and disease are a farmer's threats. You have threats, too: competition, market noise, shifts in the economy, turnover, churn, etc.

In the Plan principle, we assigned all the revenue targets to accounts. The principle closed with this sentence: *A poor sales team structure makes good performance impossible, no matter how good the sales leader or sales plan may be.*

If you are tending your revenue with a geographical territory model that divides the market solely by geographical boundaries, not by customer buying patterns, then you aren't producing the best results.

First, Understand Why Customers Buy

The geographical territory model assumes that location is essential to the customer's buying decision. But, as you'll see, proximity is no longer a requirement. Let's begin by understanding why today's customers buy goods or services. The factors that lead to a transaction have forever changed, and as a result, the way we sell also has to change.

The Buy-Sell Hierarchy (right) is the best model to help understand why customers buy in an era when it's easier than ever to find information that influences the purchase decision. It evaluates your relationship with your customer — and, more important, how your customer views your company as a partner. According to the Buy-Sell Hierarchy, firms that make an important contribution to a customer's business or organizational issues are less susceptible to pressure from price, competition, and features and benefits.

At Level 1, you're merely delivering products or services that meets bare-bones requirements, and the customer will be quick to seek newer or cheaper alternatives. At Level 4 or 5, the customer views your products and services as essential and sees your reps as an extension of their business.

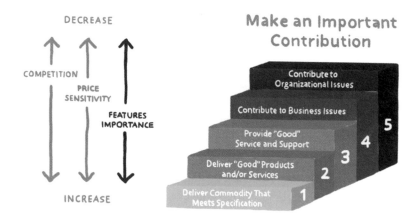

Buy-Sell Hierarchy from The New Successful Large Account Management by Robert Miller and Stephen Heiman.

Let's look at Southwest Airlines. It's my favorite airline, by far. I rarely fly other airlines, even when Southwest isn't the best option (flight times, fares, and duration). They don't charge for baggage or to change my flight, and if there's room for me on an earlier flight, then they let me switch without any hassle. On top of that, they have a companion pass (which can be earned by accumulating points) that allows my wife to fly with me for free.

My decision to do business with Southwest was more about a philosophical alignment and had little to do with cost, plane technology, number of active airports, pilot training, first class seats, or any other factor.

But Southwest isn't helping me solve any business problems. Southwest Airlines isn't providing a service that makes me a better sales consultant for my clients. By that measure, Southwest Airlines is a Level 3 provider.

So what characterizes Level 4 or Level 5 service?

Accounts are a company's external assets. Without accounts, there's really no business. Sustaining a competitive advantage today means understanding that the relationships between your customers and your company — not revenue, per se — provide the key to survival. You also need to understand that *value perceived by the customer is the only kind of value that counts.* To deliver this kind of value, you need more than a great product, more than a reliable service, and more than fair pricing. You need stellar sales reps. Above all, you need to track the changing business conditions of each customer, and then align all your resources to address their needs as only your company can. Leveraging your strength in this way is your only real competitive advantage.

Companies that tend to their customers' business needs will prosper over the long term. In order to tend to your accounts well — and thus maximize your revenue harvest — you must fully understand their business situation and needs. Next, you must perform a rigorous, team-based assessment of all the key elements that affect your customer relationships, both now and in the future. Evaluate the following:

- What initiatives will best enable the customer to maximize their opportunities?
- How can your internal resources be deployed to help the customer seize those opportunities?
- How will both your company and the customers measure the success of these initiatives?

This is how B2B selling is done in the modern era. This is how you distinguish your company from the crowd and become a Level 4 or Level 5 provider for your accounts. This is how you maximize your revenue harvest.

Note that *none of these considerations involve location.* Where you are, where your reps are, where the customers are — geography does not matter.

Tending to Your Turf:
Redefining Sales Territories

It's not about location. And yet too many companies allow geography to play a bigger role than it should when segmenting the customer base. What is a territory … really?

In its simplest form, the sales territory is an area of responsibility for an individual or team of salespeople by which sales are expected. Not Los Angeles. Not Cincinnati. Not the Midwest. The territory model is no longer the optimal structure for maximizing your revenue harvest. More importantly, it doesn't create value for customers. Many companies have moved away from a geographical territory model because it no longer places them in a position to win the most market share.

The role of a sales team hasn't changed. Sales teams create revenue by identifying and realizing opportunities to create value for customers through a series of exchanges and interactions.

In a modern market where competition has never been as fierce, where customers have never been more informed about their problems (and your solutions), it's time for you to consider a new sales team organization and deployment strategy, one that places emphasis on adding value to customers by solving their problems. Account management is the solution.

If your sales team is missing target, or tasked with scaling quickly, then it's time to re-examine the role of the sales professional (and the sales team) in achieving sales and corporate objectives. Implement account management into your sales team so that you can more consistently hit your targets in the selling year.

Sales teams that move from territory management to account management:

- Nurture deeper relationships with their customers (in fact, many customers will view your business as an extension of theirs)
- Better understand where the business is being generated
- More consistently deliver at or above forecast because account management allows reps to ramp up faster and sell more stuff

Account management isn't a strategy just reserved for large, enterprise sales teams. In fact, it's most impactful for sales teams that need to scale quickly. It doesn't matter if you have a sales force of six or 60, account management can help you scale smarter and faster.

Why the Geographical Territory Model Doesn't Work

"We need a sales rep in New York, Chicago, and Los Angeles." That's the answer I received from a B2B sales leader on a recent consulting assignment. Her argument was that these three markets represented a significant percentage of the population, and that her team couldn't possibly hit its targets without sales coverage in the larger markets.

You've used this logic to defend your hiring strategy and team too.

I asked her how much business the company was currently earning in each of these three markets. The short answer was that she didn't really know. I continued to probe. How much opportunity exists in each of these markets? By her logic of population density, the opportunity was endless. But population density of a geographical market really isn't a factor for how B2B customers make decisions to buy products and services.

It's true that New York, Chicago, and Los Angeles have a disproportionately higher number of companies (potential customers) than markets like Des Moines, Albany, or Fresno. I questioned her further, and I could see we were making progress.

I asked:

- What specific accounts in these three markets would make a meaningful contribution to your team's quota attainment?
- Of these accounts, how many are existing versus how many don't currently do business with your company and need to be qualified?
- What specific activities do you expect a sales rep to perform in these markets?
- If any of these three sales reps were to be successful at the end of his or her first year, what would that look like?

We opened the CRM and spend some time reviewing her data. We discussed the performance of each of her current sales professionals. We looked at her sales forecast for the next 12 months. By the end of our meeting, she was convinced: She didn't need sales coverage in these three large markets to hit her target. Instead, she needed to close a very specific number of accounts — regardless of where the account was located — that matched the ideal account profile of the company.

This is a common mistake sales leaders make when they structure their teams. Many sales leaders still subscribe to an antiquated model that overemphasizes the role geography plays in whether or not a potential customer will transact with your company.

The premise of the territory model is that:

- Customer bases are widespread
- Local and regional nuances are more important than national standards
- Frequent in-person contact between the buyer and sales rep is required

It used to be an absolute truth that a territory model was advantageous because it reduced travel time and expense. That's no longer true for many organizations, but many sales teams are structured by this old approach.

Plus, all territories are bad — just ask your sales reps. The territory model can limit a rep's ability to develop new business, which slows scale and traction. Some reps end up with too few opportunities, some reps with too many. The leader thinks the rep (territory) is performing well without any insight into which accounts and how much business is being lost or overlooked.

What's more, territory management:

- Skews a manager's ability to measure a sales rep's true performance
- Overlooks prospects that lie outside the geographical territory, thereby missing sales
- Is often a sign of lazy or thoughtless sales leadership

Technology Makes Location Irrelevant

Technology has forever changed B2B selling. Furthermore, technology coupled with the ease and affordability of travel (yes, it's still expensive) have made prospects more accessible.

Technology and Your Customers

More important: Prospects know more about your company and your offering than you think they do.

Maybe it's true that they don't know much about your company's specific spin on an offering, but they undoubtedly know more about the problem your offering solves than you think they do. Customers are experts on the subject of their problems. Today's customers are more informed than ever before. They spend more hours researching potential solutions before establishing contact with you, even when the source of their research is your company's content. For many selling organizations, the majority of closed deals come from prospects self-identifying with your offering before the salesperson makes contact (lead forms, blog posts, emails, etc.). The fact that inbound leads continue to increase for many B2B sales teams is proof that the customer is more informed than ever.

Since the customer has already reached some level of certainty that your offering will solve problems for their business, many times the decision to purchase or not comes down to factors beyond the offering's features and benefits.

For many of today's buyers, technology has eliminated geography from the decision-making process.

Technology and Your Sales Team
I remember a time when most of my prospecting was done in the customer's office. Today that's rare. Most of today's prospecting, discovery, and "are we a fit?" work happens through video conferencing. While it's sometimes harder to connect and build rapport over a video call than it is in person, the advantages of technology far outweigh the pitfalls.

Early in my selling career, driving 3-5 hours for an hour-long meeting was common. I'd get up in the middle of the night and drive so that I could have a few meetings in a different city, only to turn around and drive back home late in the evening. It made for some long days and weeks. Today's sales professionals can have 10+ good meetings in a single day, without any travel. Technology makes this possible.

Technology has also allowed the selling professional to be more organized, informed, and effective. CRMs, social selling platforms, data sources, and sales enablement tools have increased the number of accounts (and transactions) a rep can simultaneously manage. In today's B2B selling market, there's no reason to limit a rep's capacity based on geographical proximity to the customer.

Why Account Management Is Better
In the Position principle, I shared my experience as a sales leader with Foundations Recovery Network. When I took the sales leader position, the company was healthy and performing well in all departments except for outside sales. The outside sales team was expected to contribute 40-50% of the company's revenue, but they

hadn't hit a sales target in a long time. The team had six sales reps across the country. Each rep had a territory defined by state lines. It didn't take long for me to see a couple big problems with this structure.

The first problem was that **roughly 30% of the U.S. geography was untouched by the existing sales team.** To make the situation worse, active customers were located in these untouched parts of the country. Do you think any of the reps called on these customers? No, they didn't know these customers existed because they weren't in their territory.

Account Management vs. Territory Management

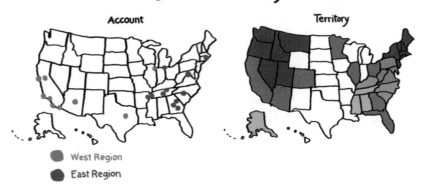

Account management = reps are assigned to a group of companies, regardless of location
Territory management = reps are assigned to a geographical region

The territory model measures sales results in the aggregate. So in theory, the territory could be "growing" **and** churning through accounts (customers). Add two new accounts in a month and only lose one, then the business is technically growing. It takes so much more effort to create a new account than it does to keep an existing account, but the aggregate increase in sales results masks the account churn problem to the sales rep and the sales leader. They see the business improving, when in fact it's struggling.

Another problem with this geographical territory model is that it **created confusion for the customer**. In B2B selling, it's common to have one customer with multiple locations.

In the situation where one account has five offices in five cities, then how does the manager assign the account? Does she assign each office to five different local reps? In a territory model she likely would. This decision could create confusion for the customer or could be entirely misaligned with how the customer wants to do business. Many companies centralize purchasing decisions and prefer to work with only one sales rep (likely the rep that initially won the business). When the account grows organically as other locations become interested in the offerings, then it begins to produce results from all five locations. Account management allows for one rep to manage this account, and to be responsible for the sales results from all five locations.

Another advantage of account management exists for sales teams that have specialized selling efforts by product. Too often, companies send four or five different sales reps into the account, each representing one specific product, not the entire portfolio of products. This structure is also confusing for the customer.

Account management is easier for the customer because he knows who to call about his business. It's easier for the sales staff because each account has one clear owner so that strategy, communication, and execution are always clear for all stakeholders. It's easier for the sales manager too, because she doesn't have to check in with five different sales reps to see what's going on with one account.

At Foundations Recovery Network, we replaced the geographical territory model with an account management model. What was the result? We increased sales by nearly 100% in 12 months without adding any additional sales representatives to the team. In January of 2013 the team closed 52 new opportunities in the month. One year later, the same sales team closed 93 new opportunities in the month.

In two and a half years, the sales team was able to triple the number of active accounts, from 212 to 760.

How Eliminating Territories Doubled Sales

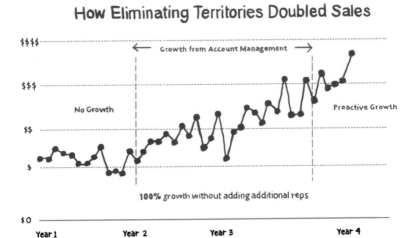

Account management isn't a new strategy. It's not a fad. In fact, *The New Successful Large Account Management*, the definitive book on the subject, was written by Robert Miller and Stephen Heiman in the 1990s. Account management helps everyone on the team have more control over sales results.

Increasing the number of assigned accounts over time should be part of every sales employee's performance review. The extent to which you track new account growth comes down to the size, maturity, and structure of the sales team. Some sales teams have reached a level of specialization where creating new accounts and managing existing accounts are executed by two different selling functions within the team. (We covered this specialization in the Plant principle.) For many companies, the number of new accounts created month over month is a key metric to track.

This is another great benefit of an account management strategy versus territory model: It applies to new, mature, specialized, generalist, large, and small sales teams. No matter how you've decided to structure the sales team, you can measure sales rep performance at the account level.

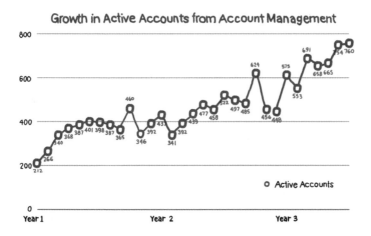

Growth in Active Accounts from Account Management

Implementing Account Management

How do you transition your sales team away from a territory model and into an account management structure? In this section you'll learn how, step by step. The transition can happen quickly too. In order to properly execute account management, many shifts are required; language is one of them.

A few years ago, I was hired by an executive team to advise a sales leader who was producing inconsistent results, at best. Her team was structured in a territory model, and she couldn't predict how reps would perform in a given month. It was creating frustration for the CEO, who wanted to quickly grow the business. Sales results could swing by as much as 50% from month to month. The sales leader needed to act quickly. And she did, making a bold decision to reorganize her team by accounts. Results happened just as quickly: Six months into the account management model, her team recorded its best month in company history. Here's how they did it.

The first thing a sales leader needs to know is where the business is coming from. Not "where" in a geographical sense, but rather which accounts are spending money with your company. An account management structure charts four key types of accounts, shown in the figure.

Types of Accounts by Stage

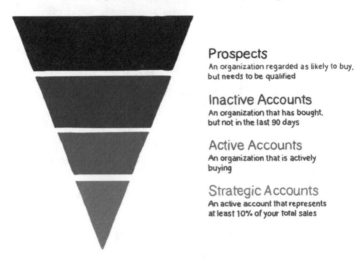

Prospects
An organization regarded as likely to buy, but needs to be qualified

Inactive Accounts
An organization that has bought, but not in the last 90 days

Active Accounts
An organization that is actively buying

Strategic Accounts
An active account that represents at least 10% of your total sales

Prospects are organizations regarded as likely to buy, but needs to be qualified.

Inactive accounts are organizations that has bought, but not in the last 60-90 days*.

Active accounts are organizations that are actively buying.

Strategic accounts are active accounts that represents at least 10% of your total sales.

Defining the inactive period is the sole responsibility of the sales leader. Only you can know how many days should pass between transactions for a healthy account; 60-90 days is a good benchmark for accounts that can transact with you on a month-by-month cadence.

In an account management model, any entity that could do business with your company is defined as an account. All accounts have a stage. Account stages are prospect, inactive, active, or strategic.

1. Open your CRM. Take a look at all the accounts.
2. Sort them by last transaction date. If there's no transaction associated with the account, then it's a prospect. If a transaction has occurred in the last 60-90 days, then it's an active account (remember, 60-90 days may not be the correct distinction for your business). If the account has bought from your company, but not in the last 60-90 days, then it's an inactive account. If the account is active and represents a meaningful percentage of total sales, then it's likely a strategic account.
3. Once you've sorted the account data in this manner, take a look at how many accounts (by stage) each sales rep owns or manages.

Number of Accounts (% of total) by Stage

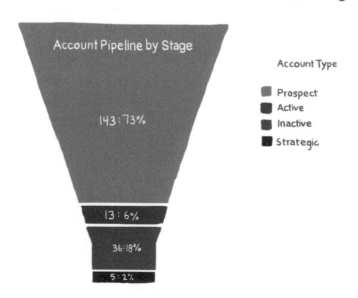

123

This should be very revealing to you. Remember, **in an account management system, a rep's territory is his assigned accounts, with little to no regard for geography**. The rep's performance is measured by his ability to increase results from the assigned accounts. Here are some questions you can expect to answer by looking at your business through the account management lens:

- How many accounts does the average sales professional manage?
- Do some reps have significantly more accounts than others?
- Do some reps do a better job of maintaining active accounts than others?
- What's your average deal size and frequency?
- How many accounts change stage from period to period?

This view of your account and sales rep performance will likely raise as many performance-related questions as it answers.

Now let's talk about reporting. You'll want to define a sales rep's territory by the total number of assigned accounts (prospects, active, inactive, and strategic). It will be important for you to track the number of accounts that move in and out of each stage, period over period.

- How many new prospects were added this month?
- How many inactive accounts were recovered to active this month?
- How many prospects were closed this month?

Compare this period's results to past period's and you will begin to see patterns in the data.

Create an accounts review report in the CRM. The report shows all accounts (by sales rep), and their associated transactions month over month. Here's a sample accounts review report:

REVENUE HARVEST

ACCOUNT REVIEW REPORT

ACCOUNTS Reviews

$ Close Date →

Account Owner (Sales Rep)	Account Name ↑	April 2018 Record Count	May 2018 Record Count	June 2018 Record Count	July 2018 Record Count	August 2018 Record Count	September 2018 Record Count	October 2018 Record Count	November 2018 Record Count	December 2018 Record Count	Total Record Count
Johnny Bravo	Atlantic Services Inc	3	4	3	5	1	4	7	6	5	14
	Bob's Plumbing	0	3	5	5	6	4	7	6	5	40
	Capital Records	0	0	1	1	1	0	1	0	0	5
	Cardinal Genetics	1	0	0	0	0	0	0	1	0	1
	Carroll & Johnston	1	2	2	2	2	3	2	0	0	14
	Dave's Deli	0	0	1	0	1	3	2	3	1	5
	Centre Lighthouse Appliances	0	0	0	1	0	1	0	0	2	3
	Acme Feed	0	0	0	0	1	0	0	2	2	1
	Clinic Smart	0	0	0	1	0	0	3	4	5	19
Subtotal		6	10	11	9	13	11	14	13	14	101
Pete Mitchell	US Technology	0	10	11	9	1	11	14	2	1	5
	Niagra Supplies	1	0	0	0	1	0	0	0	0	4
	Medical Institute	3	3	3	2	0	1	0	0	0	12
	DuPonte	2	1	2	2	1	2	2	2	0	5
	Pinnacle Lumber Yard	0	0	0	1	0	0	0	0	1	8
	Greene Labs	1	1	0	0	1	1	2	0	1	4
	Griffith Studios	0	1	0	0	0	1	1	1	1	4
	Greenwood Grocery	0	1	0	0	1	2	2	2	0	7
	Halifax Home Care	0	0	0	1	1	1	1	1	1	7
	Leopold Machine	1	0	0	0	0	0	1	1	1	4
	Ballast Point Brewery	0	0	0	0	0	2	1	2	1	7
	Stumptown Roasters	0	0	1	1	0	1	1	0	0	7
	North Bay Mechanical	1	0	1	0	0	0	0	0	0	7
	Ottawa Steel	1	0	1	1	0	4	3	0	0	10
Subtotal							11	10			71
Nick Bradshaw	DC Hydraulics	9	9	9	4	4	11	10	7	8	71
	Mental Health Alliance	0	0	1	1	2	1	2	3	5	15
	General Hospital	0	0	1	2	2	1	3	4	5	18
	Marine Adventures	0	1	0	0	1	2	2	1	1	6
	Coal Unlimited	0	0	0	0	1	2	2	3	3	10
	Coastal Health Services	0	0	0	0	0	0	0	1	0	2
	Acme Police Department	0	0	0	1	0	0	1	2	3	7
Subtotal		9	2	2	5	6	7	10	12	15	59
Total		15	21	22	18	23	29	34	32	37	231

You also need to create an *account rotting report*. This report shows, by rep, the number of active accounts at risk of becoming inactive in the coming weeks or days. It creates an opportunity to intervene. Look at the sample accounts review report to identify some rotting accounts. Look at Pete Mitchell's account set. Ottawa Steel, Greene Labs, DuPonte, and Medical Institute are rotting. If they don't transact in the next 30 days, then they will no longer be active.

Now, let's discuss how the account management model will improve sales management practices and sales team performance.

Account management is best executed by two important management rhythms:

1) Accounts reviews
2) Strategic account plans

Accounts reviews are short-term focused and cover all accounts assigned to a sales professional. Accounts reviews should be conducted monthly, individually, with every member of the sales staff.

Strategic account plans are long-term focused and written by the sales professional. These plans are reserved for the top-performing accounts and prospects. Each plan requires input from multiple firm leaders. They are time intensive and should only be reviewed quarterly.

Accounts Reviews

The first important thing to note about an accounts review is that it's a formal performance appraisal for the sales representative. *Use the accounts review report created in the CRM to guide this conversation.* For larger sales organizations with multiple layers of management, the frontline reps should do their accounts reviews with their direct manager. Then the frontline sales managers should compile the data from the sales reps and conduct a review with their leaders. Keep rolling up the accounts reviews through the layers of management until all are accounted for to the team's leader.

The purpose of an accounts review is to provide an opportunity for the sales professionals to keep the leadership team abreast of changes with customers and competitors, improving both sales performance and overall corporate performance. In addition to providing valuable information, the other key objectives of accounts reviews are to define success metrics for specific customers, to ensure that resourcing is adequate, and to monitor progress toward targets at the account and rep level. Accounts reviews allow for an individual salesperson to provide regular updates on his total set of customers. These are brief, regular updates that focus on the short-term (30 day) view. Since the reviews are held regularly, usually monthly, keeping preparation to a minimum is important. Conduct accounts reviews in the middle of the month.

The sales leader should use the accounts review report to cover all of these topics with a primary focus on sales performance to the current and next period targets committed in the forecasts.

Structuring the Meeting
What does it look like?

- **A platform for communication.** The accounts review is a forum for a salesperson to present an overall view of her accounts and prospects. It provides an opportunity to post progress to targets, request corporate resources, influence timely decisions, and highlight important issues.
- **Status of strategies for closing new business.** Conversation should focus particularly on high-potential opportunities, those the rep believes could become active or strategic accounts.
- **Next actions/resources needed.** The review begins with the status of actions from the last review and ends by summarizing actions for follow up.

Five questions a sales rep should expect to answer 24 hours before the meeting:

1. What were your key accomplishments from last month?
2. Did you experience any disappointments, concerns, or problems?
3. What will be accomplished next month?
4. Do you have suggestions to improve the team's effectiveness or the business as a whole?
5. What do you need from me?

These questions are intentionally open ended so that the responses can facilitate a dialog between rep and leader. Here's the insight you can expect to gain from each question:

What were your key accomplishments from last month? With this question, you're looking to learn about the closing of a big account or opportunity. The sales professional should highlight important meetings she conducted. Most important, did she hit her targets?

Did you experience any disappointments, concerns, or problems? If she didn't hit her targets, then you want to discuss it here. If the rep lost a big opportunity you were counting on to hit your targets, then you need to discover that here too. This is also the time to discuss organizational, market, and competitive problems.

What will be accomplished next month? In this part of the meeting, you simply want to know if you're going to hit your targets or not. Since this question is about next month, and you're halfway through the current month, it's a good opportunity to stress-test a rep's forecasting ability. Look back at the previous month's notes. Did the rep state he would be at plan this month? Is he? You're using this question to get a sense for how well a rep is in control of his business.

Do you have any suggestions to improve the team's effectiveness or the business as a whole? It's not okay for a rep to come to an accounts review without suggestions to improve the team. If she doesn't have any, then she is likely checked out or doesn't feel comfortable sharing uncomfortable information with you. Both are unacceptable. Dig in and figure out what's going on.

What do you need from me? Again, it's not okay for a rep to come to an accounts review and not need anything from you. If he doesn't need anything from you, then he is likely checked out or doesn't feel comfortable sharing uncomfortable information with you. Both are unacceptable.

One of the main reasons you should conduct the reviews in the middle of the month is because of questions 1 and 3. Waiting to conduct the review until the middle of the month gives the company time to close out the previous month, so there's certainty around each rep's results. Another benefit of doing accounts reviews in the middle of the month is that you are halfway through the month and have a better view of progress toward next month's committed forecast. Remember, you asked the rep question 3 last month. Is he close to delivering on the forecast he committed to 30 days ago?

The accounts review is a pipeline, deal, activity, and performance review — all in one.

Ask Your Sales Reps to Lead the Accounts Reviews

This is the salesperson's meeting, so she should set the agenda and run the meeting. Don't let the meeting last longer than 30 minutes. It will be difficult to accomplish this at first. Set an expectation with the team that keeping the meetings brief is important. Seek permission to cut them off when explanations are too long or you veer off topic. Over time, everyone will become more accustomed to the hard stop, and the meetings will run like a finely tuned machine.

How many times have you told a sales rep, "You need a plan"? It's easy for a sales professional to spend so much time working *in* their accounts that they never work *on* their accounts. Good sales reps have a published annual sales plan, monthly sales plan, and a weekly agenda. If they don't already meticulously plan their work, then the accounts review forces the reps to think strategically, plan, and communicate plans. It's a professional development opportunity for you and your reps.

The absence of account-level planning means you're actually planning to lose your top accounts. Seriously. Successful salespeople plan accordingly, and that includes planning for (and expecting) growth within each and every account. Forcing the reps to lead their accounts review meetings holds each of them accountable to their piece of the harvest.

Most sales plans fall short in that they don't assign the plan's growth goals to the accounts that can yield that growth. (Remember from the Plan principle that you're allocating the entire year's sales plan to specific accounts.) Accounts reviews force the sales reps to assign their targets to specific, assigned accounts.

Documenting Accounts Reviews Results

Monthly accounts reviews are the best way to collect data for a rep's annual performance assessment (covered in the Performance Appraisal appendix). I've been asking these five accounts review questions for about 10 years, and the answers to these questions will tell you all you need to know about a rep's performance.

When you reach the annual performance review, the information contained in these monthly accounts reviews will provide the basis for effective coaching sessions and will alert you to problems that you might not be aware of. And the quality of the monthly accounts reviews submitted by each sales rep, along with their completeness and timeliness, will give you useful information about how the rep is doing her job.

> *"The truth is that sales reps write their own reviews every day, when they do the activity that's required of them or not; invest in becoming trained on the product or not; learn the market and competitive landscape or not; meet or exceed quota or not. The sales leader merely serves as a journalist of sorts, documenting the day-to-day behavior and accomplishments of the sales staff."*

Strategic Account Planning

Without a solid account plan in place for each of your top-producing accounts, your selling efforts will be unfocused and scattered, which will result in limited sales growth, exposure to competitive threats, and a poor revenue harvest. If a sales executive has 30 accounts, she's tempted to treat them all the same. But they really aren't the same at all. Odds are, 50% of her business comes from just a handful of her accounts. Customers are notoriously unequal.

Once you know which accounts are most important to your business, then it's time to start managing them differently. The best way to get the most from these select few accounts is to execute a strategic account plan (SAP).

Defining and Identifying Strategic Accounts
The Pareto principle states that, for many events, roughly 80% of the effects come from 20% of the causes. This concept holds true for many companies' account base.

Strategic accounts: the roughly 20 percent of accounts that account for 80 percent of a company's revenue.

As the sales leader, you are responsible for the harvest. So your time should largely be spent tending to key relationships with the 20% of accounts that are integral to the success of your company. Sometimes it's 60:40 or 70:30; sometimes it's 90:10 or 95:5. The exact ratios aren't as important as the principle. What is most important is to know which accounts generate the most results for your company and to build a plan to maintain the business and deepen those relationships.

It's tempting to overlook strategic accounts when business is humming along, but they require constant tending. That's the function of the SAP. It digs deep on each major account, taking a long-term view (typically 12 months out) while cataloging the history and results of the relationship. SAPs provide a framework for the decision-making process for the account, document transaction history (sales by period and product), and serve as a tool for forecasting future sales performance.

SAPs take a lot of work, so make sure to get agreement from all participants before asking a salesperson to create a plan. Given the effort required, this process should only be focused on those few customers that drive the business, typically no more than five per salesperson. As you begin the process of identifying your company's strategic accounts, think about what questions best reveal which accounts meet the criteria. Factor in current value — but also look at what value might be added by an account over time. SAPs aren't just designed for current accounts. Writing an SAP for an important prospect might be the difference in winning or losing the business. Remember, the SAPs are only reviewed quarterly.

Strategic Account Plan Objectives

Strategic account planning requires you to look at how an account could benefit your business in ways other than just sales. The SAP process has three major objectives for the business: 1) to set stretch goals for each of the strategic accounts; 2) to reinforce the importance of executive relationships; and 3) to incubate new offerings. Let's further explore these three objectives.

Set "Stretch" Goals

Take the opportunity to stretch your team's thinking by setting account-specific goals that are considerably larger than current expectations. A stretch target drives the team to get creative when proposing opportunities and offerings. An example stretch goal could be securing a sole-source agreement or committed contract. Other stretch goals could be penetrating a new division or closing a new offering.

Of course, total sales volume is an important element to the SAP. It's easy to know which accounts spend the most money with your company, but the process of managing a strategic account should scrutinize other areas of business besides revenue. Evaluate relationships within the account (number of buyers and quality of interpersonal relationships), and consider competitive threats, key advocates, and unexplored areas of the account. Remember the Buy-Sell Hierarchy. Stretch goals drive initiatives that escalate your company's position up the hierarchy. You should be a Level 4 or Level 5 provider in **all** strategic accounts.

Drive Executive Relationships
Executive relationships are defined as leader-to-leader interaction. Find time for your CEO, COO, and other important leaders to connect with the customer's top leaders. **You never really appreciate the importance of good executive relationships until they are needed, and by then it is too late to develop them.** Ask your executives to schedule time to meet with the leaders of your strategic accounts to demonstrate how much you care about your customer's business.

Source for New Product Development
Well-chosen "stretch" targets will uncover opportunities for new offerings. These initiatives, as approved by the executive team, will help you secure your position within the account. This process should stress your team's ability to think, write, and work cross-functionally in ways that other competitors can't or won't.

In addition to these three objectives, building SAPs is a great way to hone the sales team's business capabilities. The ability to plan is a key management skill. The insight you gain while evaluating your team's participation in strategic planning will be helpful when evaluating staff for promotion. The company's sense of team will also be enhanced as a result of the cross-functional work required to execute each SAP.

The long game for you is to master communication between different factions within your company and your strategic accounts.

Strategic Account Plan Execution
Often sales teams will execute an SAP initiative by coming up with creative ways to impress and generate enthusiasm among the most valued clients. This may take the form of overpromising and underdelivering for a customer. Your manufacturing or delivery divisions may not have the capacity or capability to fulfill a new product or expedited service. So it's essential to involve representatives from other divisions that will be tasked with carrying out the initiative before you draft an SAP that calls for new products or services.

Like accounts reviews, it's the salesperson's responsibility to prepare and present the SAP to the leadership team. Because SAPs are designed for long-term sales success, they should only be reviewed quarterly. It should take about 30 minutes to review a single SAP, and you should schedule a salesperson to present all his SAPs in one session, because it's less disruptive to his selling efforts.

Executives should plan to communicate with every strategic account each quarter. Managers and VPs, it's your responsibility to coordinate executive communication with your top accounts. Make the introductions and get the meetings scheduled.

The fastest path to a killer revenue harvest is to exponentially increase the sales within your top accounts.

Pulling Account Management Together

When you shift your team from a territory model to an accounts management model, expect to see results in 90 to 120 days. You will see an improvement in accountability and strategy from your team. This model forces them to think and take ownership of their results. As you know by now, the effectiveness of the account management transition is contingent on how well you enforce the new procedures. Account management will help you find out what is actually happening in the business at the account level and uncover new insights about your business.

Here are five common questions that you need to tend:

How many new customers can your team create in a period? New business development is a key success factor; it's every rep's job to bring in new business. The number of new active accounts will tell you who is selling versus who is managing existing accounts.

What is the average sales volume per account? Bringing on new accounts is required. However, you want your team focused on accounts that can produce average-or-better results. Otherwise, they are wasting sales efforts that should be deployed on larger accounts.

How many accounts does it take to get to 80% of goal? This metric will let you know about how many accounts a rep can effectively manage. It informs how you hire and how you specialize the team. This metric also tells you ...

How many accounts does it take to make up the other 20% of the goal? It's important to know if the last 20% of goal is harder to attain than the first 80%. If your team is spending more time on the last 20%, then they need to see how much easier life would be if they spent less time on smaller accounts and instead focused on: 1) developing larger accounts and 2) getting more business from the accounts that make up the easier 80%.

How quickly do prospects move through your pipeline? How many interactions does it take on average to take an account from prospect to active? For many companies, it takes multiple meetings to close an account. Track this at the rep level, because it will show you the qualitative metrics of each rep. Reps that take longer or have slower pipeline velocity are likely struggling to communicate value.

Once you can answer these five questions, then hitting your number becomes more science than art. It's just a math equation. You've mastered tending. You'll hit target more consistently, and you'll feel more in control of your business. You can even expect to grow when the competition is slowing down.

Tending to Your Time

Once you've planted your people and opportunities, the way you tend to each aspect of your job as sales leader becomes critical to a successful harvest. You've probably had seasons where it didn't feel like you were managing your time well, and your numbers lagged as a result. If you spend too much time on activities that don't tend to the field, then the harvest will suffer.

No two sales managers have the same weekly schedule. Some function as the company's closer, flying around and helping reps ink big deals. Some spend most of the day reviewing reports and data, with little time to spare for actual human interaction. From company to company or even week to week, your schedule will vary. To properly tend to your schedule, you must balance three priorities: the business, the team, and the customer.

The Business

Any task or responsibility that does not relate to spending time with accounts or a sales professional is "the business." The business requires expense management, technology, human resources, forecasting, and any cross-department meeting. Yes, you have to tend to the business, but you should minimize the time your team spends on these functions. Sales professionals should spend 90% of their time with customers or trying to be with customers. For a true sales leader the business is the hardest segment to attend to. If you are reading this and find yourself enjoying the business work the most, then you should have an honest conversation about your future as a sales leader. Focusing on the business is just as important as the other two, but you shouldn't enjoy this responsibility more than your team or your customers. The business exists to support the customer and the team, not the other way around.

The Team

Don't confuse "team time" with "customer time"; if you are with one of your reps for a field ride or shadow day, and all of your time is spent with the customer, then your time should be categorized as customer time. Working on the team involves coaching on opportunities for improvement, assessing performance, and helping each sales professional get from here to there. Make time on the road or at the end of the day to coach the rep you're traveling with.

The Customer

It's also your responsibility to know the customer. If you don't have a relationship with key accounts, and a rep leaves (and they all do at some point) the business can suffer. It's important for sales managers to dedicate time to customer interaction. Spend time with prospects and mid-level accounts, not just big strategic accounts. This is also the best way to keep your finger on the pulse of what's going on in the market. Relying solely on our team's perspective is a dangerous position. Stay relevant and spend time with customers.

How much time you spend on each priority will depend on your business. If your business requires more interaction with the product team, then you will need to shepherd your team away from business tasks. You can't afford for salespeople to spend time on things that don't produce revenue. Take it off their schedule and help handle those aspects for them.

Try to spend Tuesday through Thursday in the field tending to customers and the team. Reserve Monday and Friday for business-related tasks like executive team meetings, IT meetings, P&L management, expense approval, vendor meetings, HR paperwork (reviews, new hire paperwork, interviews), etc. That schedule sets you up for success by helping you spread your time between your three most important priorities.

Here are some questions to consider:

- Is account management a better business management system for your sales team? If so, how will you introduce the concepts to your team?

- How will you incorporate accounts reviews into your performance management system? What piece of technology can you use to make the accounts review process seamless?

- Have you identified which accounts are strategic? How many do you have? Who will write the strategic account plan for each account? How are the strategic accounts distributed by rep? Do some reps have too many or too few strategic opportunities?

- How will your schedule change in the upcoming year so that you can manage the team, the customers, and the business?

With time and tending, your team's efforts begin to pay off. The energy shifts. Deals start closing. The *harvest* arrives. Let's turn all the hard work into revenue.

Principle 6

HARVEST

"And let us not grow weary of doing good, for in due season we will reap, if we do not give up."
— Galatians 6:9

Everything you've read and applied thus far has prepared you for the harvest. You're reading this book because you want to consistently harvest more revenue. For farmers, the harvest marks the end of a growing season. It's the culmination of months of work, filled with long days and periods of adversity. The quality of the harvest will determine a farmer's success or failure. A good harvest makes all the planning, positioning, preparing, planting, and tending worth the effort. A poor harvest will affect the farmer's income, decrease the amount of food available for consumption, and could also negatively affect the economy of a country, especially if it is dependent upon agriculture.

For you, a good revenue harvest means everything.

Company success: The company grew and hit its targets, and the executive team and board are pleased. Employees in other departments will have jobs next year and maybe even get a bonus.

Team success: All the long days on the road paid off. Commission and bonuses are paid, promotions and recognitions are awarded. Confidence builds in their leader, their company, their career.

Individual success: You'll get the financial reward. But don't expect a victory lap for your success. A good year means you live to fight another year. Successful harvests are your professional identity.

A bad harvest will be detrimental to your company and its employees, the team, and your career. The quality of a harvest is just a proxy for how well you and the team executed the other principles in this book. As the farmer tends the crops, he can see the crops mature. As he processes all the signs, he begins to forecast in his mind whether it's going to be a good year or not.

Harvests Aren't Guaranteed

You understand that unexpected circumstances can prevent a successful harvest. But even when you and your team have done everything possible, the yield may not match the effort. That's because harvests aren't a sure thing. If they were, chances are, there would be no need for sales and marketing. That doesn't mean that a successful harvest is just a roll of the dice, however. Executing each of the previous principles well provides you and your team an opportunity to harvest. Too many teams expect a harvest without doing the required work.

Self-interested leaders — and their teams, by extension — are focused only on making the sale and hitting a number. That's how they earn commissions. They don't follow the steps necessary to yield a solid harvest.

Deal-making leaders — and teams focused only on closing — ask for the business without doing the work that earns them the right to the sale. They don't follow the Buy-Sell Hierarchy (see the Tend principle) and create enough value for the customer. They don't solve business problems first. They ignore the real challenges that prospects and customers face, and ask for the business anyway. They believe they are entitled to the harvest.

Farmers aren't that naive, and neither are you. A world where you and your team can consistently hit your targets without following the principles of this book doesn't exist. Don't expect this principle to teach you new closing tactics. Rather, expect to be reminded that there's no substitute for doing the work, and just because you did the work, the market doesn't owe you, your team, or your company anything. It's a privilege, not a right, to be a consistent harvester.

Instead, you will learn:

- How to identify harvest seasons
- How to know if you've earned the right to harvest
- How to ask for the business with dignity
- How to manage your executive leadership's harvest expectations

Identifying Harvest Seasons

Hang around farmers long enough and you will learn about the harvest moon. One thing that sets the harvest moon apart from other full moons is that it's not associated with a specific month, as the others are. Instead, the harvest moon relates to the timing of the autumnal equinox. This means that the harvest moon can occur in either September or October, depending on the lunar cycles. So what's unique about the harvest moon? It provides an abundance of bright moonlight early in the evening, which aids the farmers and crews harvesting their summer-grown crops. Farmers take advantage of the light so that they can work longer hours and quickly harvest their crops, preserving all the year's hard work.

Harvests can't be forced, but they typically occur in a predictable time frame. You must know when to harvest. There's always a window. Every day that's too late costs you and your company.

Do you know the harvest seasons for your business?

Can you harvest ...

Every day?
Every month?
Every quarter?
Once a year?

Most companies can close a sale every day of the year. These companies have multiple offerings and a large enough account base that revenue is harvested daily. However, some products or services are only offered at specific times of the year. They could be seasonal or promotional offerings, or sometimes availability is limited due to manufacturing constraints. Maybe your customers only buy once a year. If that's the case, your harvest seasons need to be measured account by account, based on the month of their contract renewal.

These nuances affect you and your team's ability to harvest. You must know how each of these factors affect your business and ensure your plan from the first principle accounts for them.

A few questions to consider:

- If you can harvest every month, are some months historically better or worse than others?
- Do you have specialty offerings reserved for certain accounts or certain times of the year?
- What role do contracts, renewals, and discounts play in your ability to harvest?
- How many of your accounts can and do buy multiple offerings?

All of these factors play a role in your ability to identify harvest opportunities and seasons. If you don't know and manage these factors, then you won't hit your targets.

Harvests Occur in the Field, Not in the Barn

Revenue is harvested by sales leaders who focus on the field, not by sales leaders whose eyes are glued to the scoreboard. Don't be Ms. Dashboard. You know Ms. Dashboard: She's always in her office preparing for a presentation to the board. She's closed her door to run activity reports and email screenshots to underperforming reps. She's busy on conference calls all day so she can't answer the phone, but she texts right back to let you know she's swamped and she'll call you later. She never does.

Yes, you have to do this type of work, but it's only part of the job. In the Tend principle, we talked about team time and customer time. Harvests require your full attention in the field with the team and with customers. If you expect to harvest every month, then be in the field every month.

What you *do* is so loud that your team can't hear what you *say*. Making good behaviors more observable makes them easier to imitate, which makes them more likely to become popular. When behaviors become popular within your team, they become a part of the culture. Do the things you expect the reps to do. When you set the harvest pace, spending all day in the field closing business, the team watches. You don't need to call and check in on reps to see if they are going to hit their targets, because you are right there with them: putting hay in the barn.

Leave the office. Close the CRM. Finish the board report at night. Get in the field.

How to Harvest with Dignity

It's a universal sales truth that if you don't ask for the business, then you won't get it. But asking for the business when you shouldn't, or when you haven't earned the right, gives you the same result: no business.

Your job as the sales leader isn't just to close deals; it's to create lifetime customer value. What's the point of closing a deal if the account leaves the next year? According to Bain & Company, a 5% increase in customer retention is equals a 30% increase in profitability. Isn't it easier to keep a happy account than it is to acquire a new one?

So much time and energy are wasted on *mastering the close.*

Insights will get your team closer to a deal than instincts or a clever pitch ever will. Ask accounts questions. Ask questions with the intent to gain insight about their business, not because you are leading them down a path of manipulation.

Good harvests start with good listening. Any other closing "tactic" lacks dignity.

Your team's sales pitch doesn't matter as much to prospects and customers as how they experience you and your company. For many companies, the sales team is the face of the organization. The sales team is the brand. Listening allows you to connect at a human level. Listening is a competitive advantage. When the customer does most of the talking, you're headed in the right direction.

When I was younger, my dad used to tell me, "Son, you have two ears and one mouth." He was trying to teach me that in any conversation, the question-to-statement ratio should be 2:1. Good listening is a crucial piece of the closing equation. But what is good listening?

Let's start with what it's not.

Good listening isn't just creating space and time for the prospect to speak. This is an essential part of closing, but just simply being quiet at the right times isn't the same as actually listening to what your accounts are saying. Typically, your sales rep is mentally planning what he wants to say next as the customer is speaking. That's not listening.

When we actively listen to a customer, completely and attentively, then we are listening not only to the words, but also the *feelings* being conveyed.

In the best-selling book *The 7 Habits of Highly Effective People*, Stephen Covey discusses how you must "seek first to understand, then to be understood." Covey's strategy reinforces the concept that your question-to-statement ratio should always be 2:1. If your sales team is spending too much time talking, they aren't spending enough time understanding.

To illustrate this point, Covey lays out his five levels of listening:

1. Ignoring
2. Pretending
3. Selective listening
4. Attentive listening
5. Empathetic listening

When I work with sales teams on closing, I focus on Covey's final two steps — attentive listening and empathetic listening — not on the pitch.

Once your team learns how to deploy these listening skills, they'll create an invaluable gift to your business and the revenue will follow.

Listening helps your customers feel appreciated, which in turn drives sales. When your team actively listens to their customers, completely and attentively, then they are listening not only to the words, but also the feelings being conveyed. They'll listen to the full conversation, not just the parts that are interesting to them (those that are about whether or not the person intends to buy).

Good listening helps your closing conversations stay on track; it helps the prospect continue considering and exploring what may be an uncomfortable reality of their business.

During these conversations with your prospects, your sales reps inevitably reach a point where they feel compelled to interrupt, to share their insight, or make their pitch. They may feel the need to affirm the customer's feelings, or may challenge the customer's opinions and push the conversation beyond its current limits. While they'll certainly need to steer the discussion toward a close, your reps may tend to dominate the conversation — which means they aren't listening. And they won't land the business.

Eight Common Responses that Signal Your Reps Aren't Listening

The only way to know if your sales reps are listening is to be in the field with them. When you are in the field with them, pay close attention to how they respond to other people in the room. How they respond will determine if they are truly listening, or instead using pauses in the dialog to plan what they want to say next.

Empathetic listening is the fastest way to close business. When your sales reps are empathetic listeners, they are no longer sales reps. They become consultants. Empathetic listening is a learned skill that requires more than just keeping quiet to hear what the prospect has to say. Let's look at eight common types of responses your sales reps might make that demonstrate they aren't actually listening.

Each of the responses below demonstrate one of Covey's first three listening levels: ignoring, pretending, and selective listening. They can derail a closing conversation in seconds.

1. Telling

Telling occurs when your rep gives the prospect an order, directs the account's next response, or issues a command. When he does this, he is ignoring what the customer is saying and pushing forward with his own agenda. As a result, the customer feels misunderstood at best and steamrolled at worst.

Prospect: *I'm not sure we're in the market for new chairs.*
Hungry Sales Rookie: *You've got to sit in our new line of chairs. They are so much more comfortable.*

2. Scaring

This tactic is employed to warn, caution, or threaten a prospective customer away from his current direction or choice. When your rep attempts to scare a customer away from a competitor so that he will sign with you, she is ignoring the reasons why the prospect made the choice that he did. This tactic rarely results in closed business.

Prospect: *We are really pleased with our current provider.*
Hungry Sales Rookie: *Did you see the recent article about your provider's lawsuit? I think they are in big trouble. I heard they might file for bankruptcy.*

3. Consulting

Consulting is an important part of being a sales professional, but giving advice, making suggestions, or providing solutions before the customer or prospect has asked for your opinion demonstrates selective listening. Save the consulting for when the customer asks for guidance.

Prospect: *One of our newest robots broke down yesterday during surgery.*

Hungry Sales Rookie: *Have you called the manufacturer and asked for it to be replaced?*

4. Tricking

A rep attempts to trick the prospect when he persuades with unfounded logic, provides figures out of context, or simply makes up success stories. Stating facts and figures that haven't been scientifically validated demonstrates that the rep is pretending to know more than he does, or worse, that he is outright lying to close the sale.

Prospect: *I'd love to see some research on the product.*
Hungry Sales Rookie: *We are working on some material, but I can tell you that 97% [or some such bogus number] of customers see a 15% improvement.*

5. Combating

Disagreeing, judging, or criticizing a customer's decision demonstrates combative behavior. When the rep ignores what the customer wants, it shows that she doesn't have the account's best interest in mind. Never argue with the decision maker.

Prospect: *I don't know if the service is actually saving us money.*
Hungry Sales Rookie: *Of course it is! Look at last month's ROI report.*

6. Stroking

Agreeing with, approving of, or praising a customer strokes his ego. There's nothing wrong with doing this when it's honest and genuine. However, if your rep says she agrees but she doesn't, she is misleading the customer and not truly listening to his point of view. This is manipulation in pursuit of the sale.

Prospect: *We decided to forego upgrading our software this year, even though it might cost us processing speed.*
Hungry Sales Rookie: *I agree. Waiting on the next upgrade is always a better move.*

7. Counseling
Counseling happens when your rep spends the bulk of the conversation reassuring, consoling, and sympathizing with your customer. This showcases selective listening, as counseling doesn't actually address the issue he raises.

Prospect: *It hasn't been a good year for our division. Profits are down 30% compared to last year.*
Hungry Sales Rookie: *Don't worry. Most of my customers are experiencing decreased sales too. You'll be fine. It's just a bad time for the entire economy.*

8. Distracting
Distraction as a sales tactic is used to humor the customer, change the subject, or make leading statements to throw her off track. Your sales reps do this all the time. They ignore what the prospect is saying, because they think they know best.

Prospect: *I noticed our spend on suture went up 58% this month. What's that about?*
Hungry Sales Rookie: *Yes, but your overall spend was down 3%, that's the important part. Let's look at the total spend report I emailed last night.*

These Responses Hurt More Than They Help

When your sales reps offer one of these eight types of responses, they derail or prevent your customers from reaching the correct resolution. Reps spend so much time thinking about how to make the sale that they don't actually listen to what the prospects are telling them. Additionally, these bad responses have a way of distracting customers from their train of thought and set the stage for an unbalanced dynamic.

When we do this, what we are really saying is, "You don't know what you're doing. Just trust me; I'm the expert."

You may be wondering if the solution is simply to ask the customer to clarify what he is trying to say.

To a customer, this can often feel like you're pressuring them or challenging them on some level. This creates an uncomfortable situation and can cause the customer to shut down, effectively ending the conversation and potentially the entire relationship. Questioning customers in this manner can actually distance them from what they are feeling. You want to understand how the business situation is making them feel.

People mostly buy because of how your offering makes them feel, not just because of what it does.

All of these responses show a self-centered, rather than a client-centered, approach to closing. Instead of exploring the situation and finding the best solution possible, now the customer must respond to the challenge your sales rep just offered. The client hasn't truly been helped; instead, she's being directed to the outcome that best supports the sales professional's interests. Better responses exist, and they signal to you and the customer that your reps are listening well.

Eight Reflective Responses That Signal Empathetic Listening

When your sales reps actually listen to your customers, they are able to respond and restate what they've heard, in their own words, to ensure they understood what the account was saying. These responses are referred to as *reflective statements*, which demonstrate active listening. A well-formed reflective statement is less likely to evoke defensiveness and more likely to encourage continued exploration. These responses not only create better dialog between customers and sales reps, but they also create a stronger overall relationship.

Simply, these responses close more business.

Now let's take a look at what the previous conversations would look like if your reps employed empathetic listening, instead of ignoring, pretending, or selective listening.

How would this change your customer interactions for the better, and as a result improve your harvest?

1. Telling

Prospect: *I just don't know if we need new chairs.*
Empathetic Sales Pro: *Okay. Your current chairs are meeting all of your needs?*

The sales professional is now listening to the statement and affirming what the customer has stated instead of telling her she is wrong. While this may not lead to an immediate sale, it can create a relationship where **when** the customer is ready for new chairs, she knows where to go.

2. Scaring

Prospect: *We are really pleased with our current provider.*
Empathetic Sales Pro: *It sounds like you are receiving excellent service from your current provider.*

Instead of scaring or intimidating the customer, the sales professional shows that he respects the customer's decision, even if it doesn't immediately lead to a sale.

3. Consulting

Prospect: *One of our newest robots broke down yesterday during surgery.*
Empathetic Sales Pro: *Oh man. A broken robot can create serious problems for a surgical procedure.*

In this scenario, the sales professional characterizes the problem with the customer without giving advice, making suggestions, or providing solutions prematurely. Providing the necessary information can prompt the customer to ask how to handle the situation, which means he is open to the rep's advice.

4. Tricking

Prospect: *I'd love to see some research on the product.*
Empathetic Sales Pro: *I expected research to be an important aspect of the selection process. What outcomes are important to you?*

This time around the sales professional doesn't make up facts or figures to trick the customer into making a decision before he's ready. She confirms that she listened to what the customer was asking and assures him she'll get the information he is seeking.

5. Combating

Prospect: *I don't know if the service is actually saving us money.*

Empathetic Sales Pro: *You aren't sure the service is living up to your expectations?*

Using empathetic listening allows the sales professional to respond to the customer's concerns in a productive manner, without getting combative and potentially losing the sale. Expect the account to share more detail about where the service is falling short.

6. Stroking

Prospect: *We decided to pass on software upgrade this year, even though it might cost us processing speed.*

Empathetic Sales Pro: *Sounds like processing speed isn't an issue for your team.*

This time the sales professional doesn't simply blindly agree with the customer, potentially misleading him. Instead, she listens to what the customer says and restates the response in her own language. This type of attentive listening builds trust in the relationship.

7. Counseling

Prospect: *It hasn't been a good year for our division. Profits are down 30% compared to last year.*

Empathetic Sales Pro: *The division's profits aren't meeting expectations.*

Instead of spending time reassuring, consoling, and sympathizing with your customer, this interaction shows that your sales professional understands his concern. By not simply trying to placate him, the rep demonstrates empathetic listening. The account might share more about his company's shortcomings, which may open up an opportunity.

8. Distracting
Prospect: *I noticed our spending on suture went up 58% this month.*
Empathetic Sales Pro: *Correct. Suture spending was more this month. Let's look at why.*

By displaying attentive listening, the sales professional keeps the conversation focused on what the customer wants to discuss.

Better Listening = Better Harvest

Most prospects won't turn into accounts. It's just basic math. Stop thinking that most companies want to use your product or service. Most buyers are really good at ignoring new trends, ideas, or novel concepts. Forcing the prospect to buy won't guarantee that you hit your sales targets. Focus more on ways to add value to the relationship, and the sales will follow. Keep "closing with dignity" top of mind during the harvest season. Just because the account isn't ready to buy when you need him to, doesn't mean he doesn't want to buy.

Business that isn't ready to be harvested won't close, regardless of how hard you sell.

"No" is the second best answer. Keep tending the opportunity.

Managing Harvest Expectations

Harvesting and reporting yield (revenue) are two different activities. How often are you expected to report on harvest results?

For many companies, harvesting and harvest reporting are daily activities for the front lines: sales reps and sales managers. Most leadership teams want to see daily results, and that's a sound practice. Let's have bad days, not bad weeks or bad months. Measuring results versus expectations in shorter intervals leaves the business less susceptible to a poor harvest.

Regardless of the reporting cycles, it's your job to control the narrative and manage your leader's expectations. Most sales leaders don't do this well. You so badly want to hit the targets and win the approval of the executives that you:

- Overpromise that the team will hit their number, when you don't really know
- Rely on hope as a strategy, thinking that if you hold off on communicating bad results, they might miraculously improve before the period ends
- Hide from the management team, and don't get in front of a bad harvest cycle

All of these behaviors are a mistake and ultimately damage your credibility as a leader, eroding any trust you've built during your tenure.

When you misrepresent the results, it not only affects your credibility, but it also damages the credibility of your leader.

When you report to the executive team, don't let their applied pressure cause you to overpromise what the harvest will yield.

Don't weigh the hay until it's in the barn.

Communicate often. Communicate honestly. If you don't know what the results will be, then don't wing it. Don't lie. Don't overpromise. Don't create a false sense of success for your executive team. Your CEO is trusting your assessment and communicating it to the board.

Whether you know it or not, the pressure from the executive team flows through you (and your communication) to the field sales reps. They feel the pressure too. No one wants to miss a target. You have to learn how to let the pressure from the top flow through you in a healthy way. If you don't, then your reps will be scared and you won't get the most from them. Results will suffer. They won't tell you the truth. Instead your team will tell you what they think you want to hear: that they will hit their target. But they won't, and you will distance yourself from reality.

Instead …

Forecasting and Managing Your Leader

Let's start with **forecasting.**

It's impossible to perfectly forecast a harvest. I've never seen a forecasting model that's totally accurate. But forecasting is an incredibly important responsibility. Forecasting isn't just about, *will we get the business?* but also, will we get the business *when we expect to get the business?* When we get the business is often neglected in a sales leader's forecast, and **missing a when** not only means missing a target, but also damages credibility just as much as not getting the business at all.

Here are two exercises that will improve your forecasting capabilities:

– Believability weighted forecasting
– Match sales process with buying process

As we discussed in the Tend principle, forecasting should be baked into your monthly accounts review meetings. Second on the list of five questions you should ask each rep is, "What will be accomplished next month?" This is the ideal opportunity for your reps to forecast what they will close for the next reporting period.

Believability Weighted Forecasting

Most sales leaders take the rep's forecast at face value. Instead, add a *believability weight* to your forecasting.

Believability weighting your forecasts takes into account how accurate your reps' forecasts have been in previous months. If a rep has a track record of accurately predicting the revenue amount and close date, then she has a high believability and you should feel confident in including her results in your forecast to the leadership team.

On the other hand, if a rep doesn't have a strong track record of forecasting, then 1) push back and challenge him to be more honest with himself and you about the revenue he expects to close *and when*; and 2) preserve your own credibility and *exclude* this revenue from your forecast until the rep improves his forecasting ability.

Good Forecasting Starts with a Good Sales Process

If your sales process isn't well defined, then you can't possibly predict why or when an account will close. A well-defined sales process that aligns with the account buying process is a good way to add more predictability to your forecasting efforts. A well-defined sales process is a stepwise series of commitments a customer makes to define their needs and the value they expect to gain from your offering. The sales process stages are based on your best experiences of winning business.

- These customer commitments *must* be "stages" or "status" in the CRM
- The sales team *must* follow the sales process
- The sales process *must* be repeatable

A well-defined sales process looks something like this:

Interested — Evaluating — Deciding — Utilizing

In each stage of the process, you should be able to identify certain activities that represent a commitment from a customer. For example, the commitment to "learn more about your offering" exhibits interest from the customer. A corresponding sale activity would be a demo or a discovery call — and demo or discovery call should be a "stage" in your CRM. You need to map sales activities by type to stages of the sales process.

Decisions about what gets included in the forecast cannot be made in a silo. It's your responsibility to not only include the reps in the forecasting exercise, but also to have them *own* their piece of the forecast. If you complete the forecast independently, you can't expect a sales rep to commit to revenue that she doesn't feel accountable to own. These behaviors are a leading reason why forecasts are inaccurate. The salesperson must be accountable for being believable and accurate.

Let's finish with **managing your leader.**

What does it mean to manage your leader during a harvest season? If you don't already feel pressure from the top to report on how the period is going to close, then expect at some point you will. How you manage this tension will define your leadership and your career. Managing your leader effectively involves:

- Committing to closing the harvest quickly at the end of the period
- Granting her access to real-time, accurate harvest data

Close the Harvest Season Quickly

Most sales leaders aim to please. This tendency can cause you to succumb to your leader's desire to declare victory before the harvest is complete. Executives sometimes lack the self-awareness to see that they are asking you to predict the future when you can't. They do this because other stakeholders, mainly the board, are asking how the month is going. You may even feel this pressure directly from the board.

Don't tell your executive team that your team will hit its target — and hope the team pulls through. Instead, commit to closing a harvest on a specific date in the next period. Most companies can close a reporting period (month, quarter, etc.) in fewer than five business days from the end of the period. Close the harvest quickly so that your leader can manage others' expectations. All the pressure your CEO puts on you is just a projection of the pressure she feels.

You need to set the expectation that you will submit a final "end of period" report within five days of the period's close. Communicate this standard to the finance team and other departments that play a role in closing a harvest. Condition your leader that you will provide her with final number as soon as you have closed the harvest.

Unhide the Harvest

Committing to a quick harvest reporting turnaround isn't enough. Don't leave your leader in the dark. Grant her access to the sales data in real time. This sounds simple, but chances are you are forcing your leader to work to find out how the period is going. Sometimes the leader has access to data, but the report is old and incomplete or from a different source. The result is that you and your manager are looking at different data and reaching different conclusions about how the harvest is going.

You need to create a report or a dashboard that your leader can access whenever she wants to see real-time harvest data. The CRM is a great tool for this report. If your leader isn't the type who's comfortable accessing the CRM, then have the report emailed to her weekly or even daily if she's more of a micromanager. It might take time to train your manager on how to interpret the report, but it's worth the investment. Spending less time talking about how the harvest is going leaves you more time to actually harvest — increasing the chances that you'll hit your number. When she can look at the harvest results whenever she wants, she will trust you more and leave you alone to work.

These two tactics will eliminate some tension between you and your leader. She will always know how the sales team is doing. You will have more time to work in the field, and ultimately, she will trust you more because you have nothing to hide. These tactics are especially critical for new sales leaders who still have to earn trust and credibility with the management team. Fast, open communication always wins.

After the Harvest Comes Restoration

The harvest is the most labor-intensive season for farmers and sales leaders. For farmers, the harvest taxes the land, the workers, and the equipment. For sales leaders, it strains the company, especially departments that process and fulfill orders. Harvesting wears on you and the team. You may not recognize it, but it's also taxing on your accounts. That's why this final principle is so important. You might be tempted to skip this principle at the end of your harvest, but be warned: Leaders who don't *restore* don't last.

Principle 7
RESTORE

"Take rest. A field that has rested yields a beautiful crop."

— Ovid

The farmer knows that a rested field produces a better crop. He knows that planting the same crop in the same ground year after year isn't a sustainable practice.

But rest is hard for sales leaders. It's especially hard for you because: 1) if you are behind plan you are fearful that any relaxing or letting up will lead to imminent danger; 2) generally the sales culture celebrates hustle and shames rest.

Rest is misunderstood in many company cultures and interpreted as laziness or weakness. But in fact, the lack of rest and restoration is a leading cause of a sales team's inability to consistently deliver results. It's also the reason why many sales leaders' careers are stalled or derailed.

I don't know how we've arrived at this narrative that sellers never sleep. It's ridiculous. Even the athletes we admire, regardless of sport, have a dedicated season and offseason. That doesn't mean they don't work year round. In fact, they do work year round, but the work looks very different. Sport has a clear end to the season, and athletes use the offseason to prepare mentally and physically for the next season. Rest to the professional isn't lying around on the couch. It's reviewing the performance of last season and taking stock of what needs to be improved for the next. If these elite performers make time to restore, then why do you think you can lead elite sales teams, hitting your numbers year in and year out, without developing the same practice?

You may be tempted to skip this principle, assuming that either it doesn't apply to you or that it's unrealistic to think you can incorporate rest into your selling year. Be cautioned that failing to apply this principle to your leadership will eventually catch up with you. If you don't apply these practices, then eventually:

- Your top salespeople will burn out and leave
- You, yourself, will burn out, and your poor performance will affect your reputation
- Your career may stall
- You'll harm your personal health and relationships

Think back to the story of Roald Amundsen's 20 Mile March in the Plan principle. Amundsen put a cap on the number of miles he would allow his team to proceed in a given day so that they wouldn't overextend themselves and become vulnerable to adversity. He didn't want the team to start a new day so tired that they couldn't perform. Too often, sales teams start a new selling year exhausted by, or still consumed by, the previous selling year. When this happens, you are putting your team at a disadvantage. You shouldn't expect the team to deliver when they are in a tired state. You can't lead when you are tired. They will quit. Even worse, they will stay and underperform because you didn't restore them.

Rest and restoration are two different activities.

To **rest** is to not use.

To **restore** is to fix or return to its original quality.

The reality is that *both* rest and restoration are required, and the best sales leaders know how and when to structure rest and restoration into the selling year. The good news is that most of the tactics we'll cover here simultaneously provide rest and restoration.

For sales leaders, rest takes many forms. It can be a vacation, shorter days, less travel, working from home more than usual. These activities may be restful, but they aren't exactly restorative. Sure, a vacation has restorative qualities, but the restoration I'm talking about is more like fixing something that is broken. Farmers fix their tools. Farmers replenish the land after the damage from the toll of the harvest.

Your tools are people, processes, and software. Your land is your accounts.

In the same way a farmer needs to restore his equipment to top notch shape after a busy harvest season, you too, have things to fix. The farmer fixes his tractor in the slow months, after the harvest. You should follow the farmer and do the same: Fix your sales team in slow seasons.

Every selling year has peak seasons and also lulls. Use the lulls to recharge, evaluate the team and yourself, and revisit the planning principles shared in this book. When you learn how to restore, you will make better use of the slow periods, your team will better respect you as a leader, and you will give your team a better chance of succeeding in the upcoming year because they aren't starting out tired and depleted.

Identify and Capitalize on Slower Periods

No leader is immune to the taxing nature of a harvest. Twice in my sales leadership career, I failed to restore, and it cost me both times. The first time I ignored my personal health and didn't eat well or exercise for months. I worked 10-12 hours a day, mostly on the phone and staring at a computer screen. I gained weight, lost energy, and ultimately my performance suffered. The second time, I traveled too much and it was affecting my personal life. My closest relationships suffered. I was always tired and never fully present in meetings. I burned out. Again, my performance suffered as a result. I've now learned how to identify and capitalize on slow seasons so that I can not only rest, but also restore my mind, body, and spirit.

Many companies operate on a fiscal year that starts in January and ends in December. The end of the calendar year is full of holiday activities. For about six weeks from the end of November through December, business slows down. Accounts aren't as interested in meeting, reps take vacations, sales slow. Because both the calendar and fiscal years end in December, the end of the year tends to be a good time to restore. The restoration coincides with the holiday season, so it's a good time to recharge, celebrate success, and train for the upcoming year.

Take a look at your selling year: Do you have months, even quarters, that tend to be slower than others? Does seasonality have an effect on your results in some slower periods?

Be realistic. If the holidays are challenging because you can't get customers to focus on your offering, then take it into consideration. Remember, we accounted for seasonality at some point of your selling year in the Plan principle. You expect that some months will be slower than others. Whether you knew it or not, you've already incorporated restoration into the plan. If you're reading this principle before the Plan principle, then make a note to account for a season of restoration as you create the next year's selling plan.

- What are the slower months in your selling year?
- How many restoration opportunities exist in your selling year?
- Are they in the beginning, middle, or end of the year?

If you have a hard time identifying slower months, then I encourage you to find a period and dedicate it to restoration.

What is the best month(s) for you to restore?

Many sales leaders allow the team's progress to plan to dictate how they will react during the slower periods. If they are behind plan, then they press to make up as much ground as possible despite the seasonal factors that contribute to slower activity. It's futile. It's like trying to rope the wind. This behavior results in burnout for the team and jeopardizes your credibility as a leader. Increasing targets during slower sales periods is dumb.

If they are ahead of plan, typically one of two behaviors prevail. Some leaders continue to press out of greed, striving to see how much ahead of plan they can get. Others check out, let off the gas, and coast through the slower periods, doing next to nothing. You can find them "working remotely" from the golf course or the beach. This isn't restoration. This is the laziness we all loathe and want to eradicate from our teams. Restoration, on the other hand, is intentional.

- How do you tend to lead during historically slower periods?
- Do you press on at the expense of your credibility?
- Do you become the unrealistic sales leader that asks the team to do things you wouldn't do?
- Do you coast and let the team's results be what they will be because you've already met expectations or are prepared to accept whatever results the team delivers?

Or are you part of the elite few that understand how to capitalize on the slower periods of the selling year? In the past, how have you used slower periods to your advantage?

When the slower periods come, our behavior as sales leaders must change. We need to use the downtime to:

- Recharge ourselves and the team with time away, celebration, and training
- Evaluate the team's performance, account performance, and individual performance
- Begin the planning process for the upcoming sales year

Resting Your Mind & Body

Why rest? One or two good years as a sales leader won't define a career. You're in this for the long game. Professionals who stand the test of time know that turning off is just as important as turning on. So rest. If you model this principle, it will encourage your team to follow your lead. Do whatever you need to do to restore your mind, body, and commitment to the team and company. I tend to read more, run more, and spend more time with friends and family during the slower periods of the selling year. Bill Gates is notorious for "thinking time" during which he takes a week-long retreat to read, write, and think. If Bill Gates can do it, then so can you.

- How do you recharge?
- Do you need to spend more time with family?
- Do you have passions outside of work that are neglected during the selling year?
- Would disconnecting for a few days or a week help clear your mind and help you recover?

The Restorative Power of Reading

Maybe you've heard the saying "leaders are readers." But are they really? Reading is a critical part of your job, and yet very few leaders "read by example." Reading during the planting and harvesting seasons is harder than during other seasons. Reading is a great practice during a season of rest and restoration. Sometimes a good book is all you need to recharge for next year. (You're reading this book so that gives me confidence that you'll agree with my position that reading is a must for sales leaders.)

Reading is a nonnegotiable for me and my teams. Reading at work is not only encouraged, but it's expected. Most of the sales strategies and management ideas that have worked for me came from a book (not just sales books). In fact, I keep some of the most helpful books in my office, accessible when I need some help. They serve as a coach, a mentor, a great source of creativity and ideas. During my seasons of rest, I revisit these books looking to recycle ideas that served me in past seasons.

Your job is to make sure you have an answer to the problems that arise in your work. The source of those answers is up to you. You can wrack your brains and waste time struggling to create the right solution. Or you can find the answer in a book or an industry publication, saving you and the company time and money.

Encourage your team to read, even at work, on the company's dime. When you have a team of readers, your job as a leader gets easier. Instead of being the source of solutions for your team, now your teammates will bring new ideas and solutions to you. They will share with you and others what they are learning and applying to their work.

Set the example for your team. Be the leader for them to follow. Be caught reading in the office. In fact, take notes, share with them what you are reading and learning. Encourage them to do the same. If you aren't already an avid reader, if you don't look to leadership, business, and sales books to solve problems and improve your performance, then you need to.

Restoring Your Leadership

Professional development is hard work. It's a practice that separates the special leaders from the mediocre. **You are the single greatest limiting factor to your sales team's success.** If you don't get better, then they can't get better. You'll hold them back.

There's a difference in 10 years of accumulated experience and one year of experience repeated for 10 years. You're nodding your head because you know that the leader you were last year likely won't be enough to lead the team this year. You know the business, market, and company have changed — and what's required of you has changed too. But if you don't identify and address the areas of your leadership that need to change, then you're just repeating last year's experience. Leaders who repeat the same experience over and over eventually get fired.

To prevent the painful experience of getting fired, I suggest you just go ahead and fire yourself at the end of every year. Spend enough time as a sales leader and you will eventually get fired. It hurts less when you fire yourself.

Fire Yourself

A number of years back, I was serving as a regional sales manager for a healthcare company. I got an email from one of my peers, Jeret. The subject line read: "New opening: Regional Sales Manager, Dallas, TX."

That was *his* job. My heart skipped a beat. I didn't even read the email. I just called him right away.

I asked, "Jeret, what is going on?"

He said, "Well, I'm fired."

I was shocked. Jeret had blown his sales goals out of the water. If *he* was in trouble, then *I* was toast. I asked him what happened.

He said, "Well, it's become clear that my region is going to demand better sales performance, improved processes, and a better attitude."

But then he explained — the company wasn't firing him. He was firing himself.

He had figured out his liabilities, and he was letting himself know that wasn't okay.

That moment opened up a leadership opportunity for me. Now, it's a habit I practice every year. (I hire myself back, too, but more on that in a minute.)

Why You Should Fire Yourself
1. It Keeps You from Resting on Your Laurels and Getting Complacent
Whatever got you to your current level of success may not be what you need to get you to the next level. If you celebrate and dance around too long in the end zone, you may lose your focus for the rest of the game.

By firing yourself, you keep yourself from becoming complacent in your own success. In my experience, it helps me stay hungry and aware that I can't move to the next level by staying where I am.

Don't get me wrong. I'm all for celebrating success. Just don't conflate that celebration with satisfaction. Don't go into the next year telling yourself, "If I just do what I did last year, I'll be fine." That kind of thinking is dangerous, and firing yourself is the best way I've found to disrupt it.

2. You Get Fresh Perspective

If you look at the 500 largest companies in the U.S., the average tenure of an executive is just 4.9 years. If you go to the NFL, a typical head coach won't last more than 38 months. It's even shorter in the English Premier League, where soccer managers coach a team for just 1.31 years on average.

What does all that matter?

First, remember that having your job shouldn't be a given. At the highest levels, you don't keep your job unless you have major success to show that you deserve to.

Second, learn from the people who beat the average. Look at longstanding leaders like New England Patriots coach Bill Belichick and Amazon CEO Jeff Bezos. What do they do? They study the competition tirelessly. They go look at other industries. They get outside of their usual framework. They talk to customers. They go solicit feedback from people that aren't as intimately tied to their business to say, "Here's what you're not seeing."

If you think of yourself as dispensable, you're going to be more motivated to make sure you're bringing *indispensable* value to your company.

3. You Give Yourself Permission to Walk Away

When you fire yourself, you can honestly pause and ask, "Am I up for another year of this?"

We have a responsibility to ask ourselves this question. And it's okay if the answer is no. Life happens. Circumstances change. New kid, new home dynamics, new values.

It's okay to go into a year and say, "You know what? I don't think I am the guy," or "I don't think I am the gal." That is a gift to you and to the company. It allows you to go be successful somewhere else and for the company to get the right person in the right role.

If you're like most people, though, that won't happen. Instead, you'll realize that you love your job deeply and believe you are absolutely the guy or gal for the job.

Most people get even more excited. It results in a level of energy and excitement about the upcoming year you never thought you would have. It's a gift that I promise you won't regret.

How to Re-Hire Yourself

Okay, so you don't have to stay fired. If you decide to stick around, it's time to hire yourself back. How does that work? Well, it's a lot like any other hire.

First, interview yourself. Ask yourself the standard interview questions. For example:

Do I have the experience to do this job well? In other words, did you actually get new experience last year? Do you really have five years' worth of experience or do you have one year's experience times five?

What would my customers say about my performance? Would they vouch for what I've done? Did we hit our sales targets? Did I manage the team in a way that makes me proud?

Do I contribute to a healthy culture? Would you hire yourself based on how you spend your time? Based on how you interact with others?

Second, rewrite your job description. Where are you the most effective with your time? Eliminate the things you were doing last year that aren't going to get you where you need to be. Think about how you need to behave differently, how you need to respond differently in the upcoming year, and what your new goals and expectations of yourself should be.

Third, accept the job. Say yes to the new challenge and pop that champagne. You're not celebrating your past success. You're celebrating the opportunity you've been given to go out and do something even greater.

Remember Jeret from my story earlier — the guy who gave me this idea? Well, he and I still do this exercise. We keep each other accountable to stick with this ritual every year.
It's an unexpected process, but it has served me well. I get priceless perspective on myself and my performance each year, and I find new levels of excitement for the challenges ahead. I hope you'll find the same when you try it.

Resting the Team

Encourage your team to rest too. You need to set the example that rest is required and expected. Share with the team how you plan to exploit the slower periods to recharge and engage in recreational activities. Encourage them to do the same. Take it one step further. Check in with each of them and ask them to tell you how they plan to capitalize on the slower periods. Make a note of who's traveling where to do what. Who's going to read what book or run which race.

Occasionally you will have a few workaholics. They don't rest well. This is when you need to force a vacation. Talk to human resources about how to best approach this practice. Some companies have a "use it or lose it" policy on vacation and specific PTO benefits. Essentially it's good for all parties if this person takes a break. I've seen too many good reps spiral into addiction, depression, and develop avoidable health conditions because of too much work.

Incentive trips are a great way to reward the team and force your top performers to rest. Top performers wouldn't dare miss out on an opportunity to celebrate the team's success. Book a trip, invite spouses and significant others, and watch the team deepen relationships with each other, fall back in love with the company, and appreciate how much you care about them.

Restoring the Team

Every year brings changes in technology, process, and unfortunately, people. It's an unavoidable truth. While these changes are necessary, implementing them at the wrong time can jeopardize the harvest. Rolling out a new CRM, deploying a new inventory management policy, and changing the commission plan during planting or harvest season are huge distractions. So why keep introducing disruptive change to your sales team during peak harvest seasons?

The slower periods are a great time to fix what's broken on the team. Restoring the team could take many different forms. Use the slower times to implement change, deploy new tools, evaluate individual rep performance, and think about succession plans.

Implementing Change

Change is the only constant for fast growing companies. Hopefully you've conditioned your sales team to expect that today's reality can change in a moment's notice. Still, you should strive to manage change in a way that doesn't distract your team. Change forces the team to focus on the organization, not the market. Every time you force the team to manage internal changes, you take away from energy that could otherwise be spent growing the business. We've all worked for companies that pivot every week or month. It's exhausting to the sales team.

To the extent you can, save these necessary changes for the slow periods. Instead of introducing new changes as the management team requests them, see if you can secure permission to introduce them at a more convenient time for the business. Position the delay as a way to keep the team focused on sales. You will find that batching a group of changes versus implementing a series of small ones keeps the team focused on growing the business and less worried about what the company is doing.

So going forward, don't roll out new technology in the middle of your busy selling year. Don't change the commission plan in the middle of planting season. If you need to move a rep to a new market, consider making the change at a time that is least disruptive to the harvest.

Assessing Annual Performance

In the Tend principle you learned that performance appraisals happen monthly via an accounts review. Sales reps write their own reviews every day — as they do the activity that's required of them or not; invest in becoming trained on the product or not; learn the market and competitive landscape or not; meet or exceed quota or not. The sales leader merely serves as a journalist of sorts, documenting the day-to-day behavior and accomplishments of the sales staff.

Assessing performance is the formal review process you use to evaluate and support sales rep performance. It is part of a system of performance management that is based on goals you and your sales reps set together. Use the time dedicated to restoring the team to conduct annual performance reviews.

Through monthly accounts reviews, you have an opportunity to see how well reps are performing relative to their goals, and the process makes the annual assessment pretty straightforward. If you can, conduct performance reviews in person. Schedule a couple of hours with each rep and bring copies of each month's accounts reviews.

Use these conversations to focus on the formal goals and performance expectations that can impact salary, merit increases, or promotions. Appraisal sessions are both a confirmation and a formalization of the ongoing feedback that should be part of every manager's relationship with her team. Performance assessments should never contain any surprises.

In order to prevent surprises, cumulative conversations are necessary.

This is why you conduct monthly accounts reviews.

(Because performance appraisal is such an important responsibility of the sales leader and it doesn't fall squarely in one principle, I've created an appendix at the end of the book dedicated to performance appraisal.)

Succession Planning

At some point, the current structure of your team will need to change. Great performers need to be groomed for more responsibility and a greater contribution to the business. Most of the reps on your team came to work for you because you promised them more. More chances to learn. More chances to advance their career. More opportunity for impact.

Use the restoration period to identify individuals you want to approach for more challenges and opportunities in the coming year. Create opportunities for these select people to apprentice. They can apprentice under you or another leader on the team. Seek ways to expose them to more leadership opportunities and get them excited about what could be available to them in a new role, should they choose to accept.

When you enter next year's planning phase, you might decide you need more sales managers. It's comforting to know who you have on "the bench." When you can develop a strong bench of talent, planning for the next year, including adversity, isn't as problematic. You have to use the slower time to apprentice. Asking a leader to have an apprentice rep during a busy season isn't fair to the leader or the rep. The leader will see the rep as a burden, and the rep will feel like a burden.

Final Thoughts

Remember that we work to live not live to work.

If we're just working all the time, then what's the point?

Hopefully you get the sense that you can have lasting success as a sales leader. The key to lasting success is balance. Building a long and successful career is a marathon, not a sprint. There will be seasons where it feels like a sprint, but you must learn to slow down when the business allows.

I've used these seven principles to guide my sales leadership, and with these principles I've shaped a rewarding career. If you are disciplined enough to apply these principles to your selling year, you can expect to enjoy successful revenue harvests for many years to come. Success isn't an accident. Quick-fix solutions and trendy tactics will only get you so far. Be like the farmer who has evolved and adapted to changes in economies, changes in technology, and changes in seasons. Be a principled sales leader, and you will stand the test of time.

Appendix

PERFORMANCE APPRAISAL

Any business manager is responsible for monitoring his team's performance and communicating to them whether or not they're meeting expectations. That responsibility is doubly important for you as a sales leader, because your team's performance versus expectations has real, significant, bottom-line ramifications. Your performance review role has three components, all of which are essential:

- 90-day review
- Accounts reviews
- Annual reviews

Is a new hire meshing with the team dynamics and working effectively to drive business? Or do you need to cut bait and find another? You won't know unless you conduct a **90-day review**. It's best practice that a new sales hire's first 90 days are a probationary period: meaning the decision to hire them full-time is being deferred to the outcome of the 90-day review. (Hiring and onboarding are covered in the Prepare principle.)

You can't skip the monthly **accounts reviews** or the annual performance reviews will be full of unpleasant surprises. You'll miss the opportunity to catch problems (like revenue targets that are in jeopardy) when they're easiest to remedy. (Accounts reviews are covered thoroughly in the Tend principle.)

Finally, if you don't conduct **annual performance reviews** for each person you manage, you're not an effective leader. Your team relies on you to offer guidance, coach them on deficiencies, help them grow professionally, and evolve into new roles. (Learn more about making time and space for annual performance reviews in the Restore principle.)

Each of these reviews happens on a different timetable and has different points of focus. Accounts reviews, as discussed in the Tend principle, revolve entirely around the rep's business activity and results for the month, and they follow a specific format as noted in that principle.

Both the 90-day review and the annual review assess the rep's performance through a wider lens. They share some action steps, which we'll cover a bit more in-depth here:

- Objectively evaluating a rep's performance compared to your expectations
- Monitoring each rep's performance and documenting your communications and observations
- Preparing for and structuring the review meeting

Objectively Evaluating Performance

Whether you're evaluating a new salesperson's first 90 days or a longtime employee's year, do so in terms that are fair and balanced. Comment equally on good performance and on opportunities to improve. Focus on key points that you can support with documentation, including:

- Documentation of sales activity in the CRM
- % to plan on key performance indicators (KPIs)
- Training and development benchmarks
- Attitude, communication, and customer service

Use a numerical scale to rate the employee's performance:

1 = Significantly underperforming
2 = Underperforming
3 = Meeting expectations
4 = Exceeding expectations
5 = Significantly exceeding expectations

At the 90-day review, a rep who scores at least a 3 on the scale is well on track to success. As you begin the conversation, reassure him that a 3 rating out of 5 is your goal — it's unlikely that the rep will reach rock-star performance status after only three months on the job. He may be taken aback by what he sees as a middle-of-the-scale ranking, so you should be clear that he's meeting your expectations.

Veteran reps are more likely to reach 4 or 5 on the rating scale. For good or superior performance, present specific details to support that rating. The more specific the feedback, the more likely the rep can repeat and improve upon the behaviors. Top-rated performance might include activities such as exceeding quota, taking on a special project, or closing a huge new account.

For performance that needs improvement, identify the cause-and-effect links between the rep's actions and attitudes and results. Does the rep demonstrate a lack of skills to do the job, or low motivation? Also ask yourself how you (or the company) may have contributed to or interfered with your rep's performance: unclear expectations and/or direction, inadequate assistance and resources.

Always refer to your company's guidelines on rating overall performance. You want to partner with human resources on all formal performance assessments.

Monitoring & Documenting Performance

Think of the review process as a partnership with your sales reps; your role is to remove barriers so the rep can succeed. Involve your reps in every stage of the appraisal process, so you can see both sides of the story. Sometimes reps aren't succeeding because of organization or operational challenges that you may not even know hinder performance. For example, a rep may be struggling to access the technology he needs to perform the role, or underperformance or poor communication from another department could be limiting his ability to perform.

Documenting and preparing for a 90-day or annual review includes the following:

- Self-assessment
- Team and culture assessment
- Manager assessment

Sales Rep's Self-Assessment

In a self-appraisal, the employee evaluates her own performance against goals and identifies factors that hindered or supported her work. She summarizes her achievements and outlines the resources that will help her succeed going forward. The format of the self-assessment can vary from just a few jotted notes to a structured written appraisal, but the important element is getting her perspective. Involving employees in the process also:

- Sets the tone of partnership in the review process
- Reduces negative reactions to feedback
- Promotes a trusting relationship between you and your reps

Team and Culture Assessment

The longer you have been with a company, the less likely you are to be aware of the surrounding culture. A new rep doesn't have that organizational blindness and can tell you honestly how you and the team really behave. The purpose of this assessment is for the newest team member to evaluate the team's culture, values, and performance. Reassure her that her comments won't affect her performance review, so she'll feel freer to be candid.

Veteran reps should conduct a culture assessment each year too. Team culture is a moving target. As you add new members to the team, they reshape the culture. Veteran reps, especially good performers, can tell you if the culture is getting better or worse as you add more reps.

Sales Leader's Assessment

Evaluating your employee's performance involves reviewing multiple sources to gather as complete a picture of the employee's performance as possible. Your review should include the following:

- The job description
- The employee's own performance goals
- Your criteria for successful performance — key performance indicators or KPIs
- The employee's history, including skills, past training, and past job performance
- Your documentation of performance observations and other relevant data
- The rep's self-assessment
- If possible, an informal 360-degree feedback — feedback from a full circle of the people who interact with the individual, which could include customers, peers, and the employee's direct reports

Document the conversations you have with her and discussions you have with others about her performance. (Consult your HR team for guidance on legal requirements regarding performance documentation.) This is especially advisable when a rep's performance doesn't meet the expectations of the role, and if you are planning to terminate her.

Preparing for the Review Conversation

90-Day Review
Preparing for the 90-day review process is just as important as the actual review. Before you extend an employment offer to a potential hire, clearly communicate that she'll begin her relationship with your company on a three-month probationary period, at the end of which she'll have the opportunity to review her performance with you. Define milestones (such as action steps, training, or results) for the probationary period that are objective, documented, and mutually agreed upon, in writing, when she is hired.

Conduct the 90-day review no later than 30 days after the 90-day mark. In a perfect world you can conduct the review on the rep's 90th day. Schedule 60-90 minutes, so the conversation is not rushed. Walk through the documents you've gathered: the assessments, outside feedback, progress toward expected milestones. Evenly balance praise and criticism, and be objective in your tone and language.

Beyond the numbers and check boxes, assess whether the rep is still excited about the opportunity, the company, the team, and you. It's your job as the leader to work through all the ways the job affects your team.

- Is he having fun?
- Is the opportunity what he expected?
- How does the work affect his personal life?
- Has he grown as a person?
- After 90 days, how does he feel about his decision to join the company?

Annual Review

Salespeople, like anyone, tend to be anxious when approaching performance appraisal meetings, so it is key that you set the tone of partnership right in the beginning. Start out with a review of the purpose and objectives of the performance appraisal and note its positive benefits for both parties. This psychologically prepares you and the employee, and it acts as a warm-up for open dialogue.

Ask the employee to talk about his self-appraisal. This helps you understand the employee's point of view and prevents you from controlling too much of the conversation early on. Listen very carefully to what he says without interrupting. Demonstrate that you are listening by repeating what you've heard.

Most reps have one or two areas of performance that need improvement. These areas should be clearly documented in the appraisal form. It's also important to establish key developmental areas the rep should focus on over the coming year. Finally, detail a plan to provide formal and informal training in these areas.

Sometimes, you'll need to terminate a sales rep's employment. If the rep has struggled, he will likely continue to struggle. Let's do everyone a favor and end the relationship on good terms. Remember, terminating a sales rep from your team is really allowing them to move on to a situation where he can be successful.

Additional Resources

For more detailed information on performance assessment for sales professionals — including document templates and sample communications — send a request to hello@nigelgreen.co.